Praise for Dead Men Talking

"*I remained engrossed at each reading of your written word. Your free-flow-ing style made the subject materials very interesting and I believe will be very attractive to non-AC'ers. You have the presentations in natural sequence with excellent biblical support. The reader will realize the ample under-girding of the Holy Scriptures, yet will not be able to escape how logical the plan of God is for his children. This would be an excellent book for Sunday school classes for upper teens through adults. I aim to place a copy in the hands of my children and my adult grandchildren when this becomes avail-able.*"

—**Rev. Glennon Balser**
Former ACGC President

"*I am so glad I had the opportunity to read your book. I have thoroughly enjoyed the experience. I now know the difference between Bible study and Bible reading. I feel like I have had real spiritual growth and better under-stand the Advent Christian Doctrine.*"

—**Joene Hall**
Advent Christian Church Member
not raised in the Advent Christian Church

"*I am pleased that you have written your book so lay persons can easily read and understand it. I think it will be a great tool to acquaint new Christians with the teachings of the Advent Christian Church.*"

—**Rev. Pomeroy Carter**
President of the Florida Conference
of Advent Christian Churches

"When dialoging with Sam about chapters nine and ten while traveling together in Africa last year, I had a feeling God was doing something significant for our denomination. The training of our local pastors in that strategic part of the world had brought our paths together again. I heard in Sam the passion to share with words and now in writing the message that God had been showing Him for several years. After reading the manuscript, I am convinced that Sam is offering an incredible gift to the Advent Christian community at large. I can envision this book being used extensively by our leaders in Africa and Europe. A concise and practical theology defining clearly a grand and revealing Biblical viewpoint for all who will give it a read. Yeah, God! Thanks for listening Sam."

—Rev. Frank Jewett
Pastor of the Oxford, Maine
Advent Christian Church
and ACGC European/Africa Area Director

"Dr. Warren has written a fresh, understandable and challenging book on the Biblical teaching of the nature of man, life only in Christ and the life to come. This book will be an excellent tool to use with new believers, new members, and Sunday school classes. It will be especially useful overseas for the training of national pastors and church leaders where much theological training is passed down through preaching rather than formal study. You have done a great job. I like its fresh and simple explanations of important Scriptures that deal with the topics of life only in Christ. I appreciate your approach of challenging people to seriously check their beliefs against the Scriptures."

—Rev. Hal Patterson
Director of World Missions
Advent Christian General Conference of America

"I have just finished reading Dr. Warren's book. What a refreshingly accurate and factual presentation of "Thus Saith the Lord!" This book is an absolute **must** *for every serious student of the Word of God and should be required reading for every prospective Minister."*

—**Rev. Dr. J. Ronald Schoolcraft**
Elder Emeritus
West Jacksonville
Advent Christian Church, Jax, FL

Your book is not deep theologically in the sense that you handled the material in an easy, familiar conversational style. Your arguments, to me, were persuasive, cogent, and sensible. I think that the questions you ask are certainly relevant and hopefully will stimulate the reader to search for the true Biblical position."

—**Rev. Laura Putnam**
Former Advent Christian Missionary

"Thank you for allowing me to read your book. I found it hard to put down. I think the presentation is clear and should be helpful to anyone who would read it seriously."

—**Rev. Luree Wotton**
Former Advent Christian Missionary

"I found your book easy to read and understand. I believe anyone with knowledge of the Bible will find your book to be scripturally sound. I liked very much the way you wrote the book, especially the personal touches. I enjoyed taking the journey with you."

—**Mrs. Alma Perchy**
Deaconess
West Jax
Advent Christian Church, Jax, FL

*"I just finished reading your book and it is **great**! There has been a crying need for a book of its kind. While other books dealing with these subjects are long and perhaps too scholarly for the "man in the street" type of reader, your*

book will fill that need **perfectly**! I believe this book will be greatly used of God to convince a person that **his** Word is true, no matter what the Advent Christian (or any other) Church teaches."

—Dr. John Roller
ACGC Urban Ethnic Ministries Coordinator and
Coordinator of the ACGC Resource Center

Dead Men Talking

Dead Men Talking

✦

What Dying Teaches Us about Living

written by
Dr. Thomas S. Warren II

Foreword by
Edward Fudge
author of The Fire That Consumes

iUniverse, Inc.
New York Lincoln Shanghai

Dead Men Talking
What Dying Teaches Us about Living

iUniverse books may be ordered through booksellers or by contacting:

iUniverse
2021 Pine Lake Road, Suite 100
Lincoln, NE 68512
www.iuniverse.com
1-800-Authors (1-800-288-4677)

ISBN: 0-595-33627-2

Printed in the United States of America

Dedicated to Linda & Gail (1949–2002):

My wonderful sisters who shared their lives with me and by their examples I have learned to live life to the fullest and make God the center of all I do.

Contents

Foreword

Inertia shows up in religion as well as in physics. That is why it is easier to go along with accepted teachings rather than to investigate the Scriptures for ourselves. For example, it is often said that every human being has a soul that is inherently immortal and can never die. As a result, popular Christian opinion holds that every soul will live forever in either heaven or in hell. It is commonly thought that those who die go immediately to one of those destinations. Death thus becomes only a transition from one sphere of life to another, the idea of resurrection loses almost all significance, and Christ's final return becomes a near irrelevancy.

"But not so fast!" exclaims author-pastor Sam Warren in this book. Are these ideas really found in the Bible, or do they come from somewhere else? Beginning with the opening chapters of Genesis, Warren walks carefully through both the Old and New Testaments as he answers that question. The biblical teaching, he concludes, is that the human being does not *have* a soul but rather *is* a soul. Death is death, not life in another form or place. God's remedy for death is the resurrection of the whole person, not a death-proof soul or spirit.

What about hell? Is it a place of unending conscious torment as frequently alleged? And how about heaven? What can the saved expect throughout eternity? The Bible's answers are surprising on both counts, says Warren. It pictures a hell that is much hotter than the popular image allows—a hell that totally burns up forever all who go there. And rather than visualize disembodied souls strumming harps in heaven, the Bible encourages us to look forward to full-bodied life in a new universe, where we will be companions with God's people from throughout history, with the Father and with Jesus Christ.

True to his promise, Warren bases this all on a careful reading of the word of God, carefully separating fact from fancy, distinguishing popular traditions from biblical teaching, in the end offering solid scriptural ground on which we may joyfully and confidently stand. Why settle for inertia when we can rely on inspiration instead?

Edward William Fudge, author of *The Fire That Consumes*

Introduction

"Don't be afraid to ask dumb questions; they're easier to handle than dumb answers!"

—Anonymous

Growing up in a pastor's home has given me a distinct perspective on the way a people develop their theology. For years I attended church, went to Sunday school, and joined the activities of the church. For the life of me I can't remember a time when I questioned the source of what the church, my parents, or anyone else taught me about God.

Looking back on these formative years I now realize how common it is for people to grow up and never question the things they have been taught. For the most part people simply absorb the information before learning to evaluate the validity of its claims. That this is an often-repeated experience has been confirmed for me after almost thirty years of pastoral ministry. No matter where I go, I continue to find people who call themselves Christians yet have little real knowledge of the word of God. People believe things largely because somebody they respect like a parent or a teacher told them that this is what they should believe. This approach to the development of a biblical viewpoint violates everything I remember learning in seminary about exegesis. The reality is that people hold to their convictions largely due to the circumstance that a teaching has been passed down through their families—especially the fathers—to each successive generation. In the end, the result is that most people do not have a clear understanding of what the Bible teaches on a given subject. Sadly, I cringe to think of the biblical illiteracy rate in the church of today.

Throughout my years in the pastorate I have met many who believed things that were never derived from a careful examination of the Bible but simply because the context in which they were raised accepted those beliefs as normative. While I recognize the importance and influence of a person's family of origin, peers, and experiences as part of one's growth and maturity, this cannot be the determining factor in interpreting the word of God. As a result, I often find that this type of person misses the natural and intended meaning of the Bible when it conflicts with their personal beliefs formed in the crucible of their life.

The extent to which this happens can be seen in the reaction within the evangelical community when confronted with the accuracy of one of its central doctrines dealing with the nature of man. In recent years, much debate has taken place regarding the biblical teaching on the subject of man's nature and the punishment of hell. Scholars like Robert Peterson, Edward Fudge, Lee Strobel, and others have faced off as to the Bible's true position on this tenet of the faith. At times the discussion has been heated. Some have resigned themselves to the position that says we agree to disagree. Others, however, have taken the view that anything other than a belief in the immortality of the soul and everlasting punishment in hell is heresy.

Having been raised in a theological tradition that supports the belief that man is *not naturally immortal*, and therefore subject to total destruction (annihilation) in the fire of hell, I wondered whether or not I held to this doctrine because I truly believed it was supported by Scripture or because Daddy told me it was so? As a result, I chose to reexamine the foundations of my beliefs. This book represents my journey through the pages of the Scriptures in an attempt to let the word of God speak for itself to the most natural understanding of the text with respect to the nature of man, heaven, hell, and the destiny of mankind without Christ.

For many, especially those who think that they believe in a certain way, this kind of study will be threatening. To entertain the thought that one's theology has been shaped more by family, friends and false teachings than the Bible is a hard pill to swallow. And, should the evidence prove it, fewer yet are willing to make such a drastic change and admit that for years they have believed something that was wrong and did not match the evidence of the word of God.

The strategy of this book is to take the reader on a journey from the beginning to the very end of the Scriptures. By doing this, I will seek to demonstrate that the most natural teaching of the Bible reveals a clear and distinct difference between God and man as it concerns their nature. It is the conviction of the author that the only way this truth can be missed is by not studying the word of God in context and not allowing the Scriptures to speak for themselves. Interestingly, Paul gave similar advice to Timothy years ago when he said, *"Do your best to present yourself to God as one approved, a workman who does not need to be ashamed and who correctly handles the word of truth"* (2 Tim. 2:15).

Will you join me on this journey? Will you take the challenge to study God's word in a search for truth, even if it turns out to be different than what you now believe? *If so, let the journey begin!*

1

Truth Handles

"Truth is beautiful, without doubt; but so are lies."

—Ralph Waldo Emerson

I will always be amazed at the ideas that are generated while discussing theology. In fact, in Bible College, sitting around the lounge late at night often brought out the best and most creative thinking. Some of the ideas were basic theological concepts, but quite often we would begin our comments with "What if..." or "I tend to think..." The fact that most of us were just beginning our journey into studying the depths of the Scripture caused most of our thoughts to be left alone and never plummeted for their consistency with the word of God.

While many good thoughts have died along the path of contemplation, the sad reality is that many Christians, pastors, and even denominations cling to their beliefs, never questioning its biblical integrity. Unfortunately, there will always be present those who develop and accept theological concepts out of preferences over against exegetical soundness.

The apostle Paul devoted a considerable amount of time warning young Timothy against the acceptance, even toleration of what he called *"myths and endless genealogies"* (1 Tim. 1:4). These ideas and teachings promoted controversy *"rather than God's work-which is by faith"* (1 Tim. 1:4). Paul described the proponents of such views as those who "want to be teachers of the law [Bible], but do not know what they are talking about or what they so confidently affirm" (1 Tim. 1:7).

I, for one, am not ready to accept everything that someone says simply because they are popular or have a degree behind their name. Millions of people have been led to believe things because it is in print, on the radio, or they saw it on television. Needless to say, this is a poor and unacceptable way to handle God's word, our source of truth.

THE TRUTH ABOUT TRUTH

The Bible is not that hard to understand, at least at its elementary level. Granted, there are subjects addressed by the Bible that need detailed study prior to formulating a clear view of its teaching. This, however, is not the case for most of the Scriptures. Paul told young Timothy to watch out for those who do away with the basics of the Bible in order to feed their own purposes. Instead, Paul demanded that Timothy do his very best to present himself as a *"workman who does not need to be ashamed and who correctly handles the word of truth"* (2 Tim. 2:15).

The particular context for this saying is quite interesting. The admonition to correctly handle the Word of truth is in an attempt to prevent the spread of heresy (nontruth). Paul states that false teaching has a way of spreading like gangrene (2 Tim. 2:17). As an example, he uses the idea generated by Hymeneaus and Philetus, who have spiritualized the historical event of the resurrection of Christ by saying that it had already happened.

A MODERN-DAY SICKNESS

Two thousand years have passed since the writing of these words to Timothy, yet the practice of misinterpreting the Scripture is alive and well today. Perhaps, none so blatant as those held concerning the nature of man and his impending future with or without Christ.

The twenty-first century has brought forth a host of books, magazine articles, debates, and countless discussions regarding the issue of whether or not man "has" a soul or "is" a soul. Who hasn't been present at a funeral or memorial service and heard the pastor attempt to offer words of comfort to family and friends alike on the eternal status of their loved one. In most cases it doesn't matter whether or not the person was saved, resulting in a type of watered down universalism. It has always been of interest to me that the same pastor or leader that offers these words of comfort does not make it equally as clear that the "lost" person is in hell, as adamantly as they put the saved person in heaven. In times like these I often wonder if truth is only truth when it is convenient.

In the spirit of Paul's words to Timothy (2 Tim. 2:24–26), my purpose is not to cause trouble or to get into an argument with those who believe differently. Rather, I simply want to accurately handle the word of truth. What does the Bible really say about the nature of man? Does he "have" a soul or "is" he a soul? Where does one go to determine the answer to this foundational question? If we are to approach this subject from the beginning, it makes perfect sense to go back to the beginning. Therefore, Genesis becomes the natural starting place for a seeker of truth. It is in Genesis that we find the beginning of all things.

2

The Beginning of the End

"The biggest difference between ourselves and others is that we don't tell half of what we know, while they don't know half of what they tell!"

—Anonymous

The book of Genesis is a book of beginnings. It is where we go when we want to understand how things started and for that matter how things went wrong. Everything we know about today can be understood in some degree by studying the book of Genesis. Not only did all things begin in the beginning, but everything that began was good. This means that what God created was exactly as he wanted it to be and there was no need to change it. In view of this, if we can determine exactly what God created, we will find the model for all of creation and history.

The pinnacle of God's creative powers can best be seen in mankind. At the end of his creative agenda we find man and woman. God had determined that they would be made in his image (Gen. 1:26) and that they would have authority over the rest of the creation (Gen. 1: 26–28). His initial activity would be to "work" the land that had been given to him (Gen. 2:5–6). God created Adam partly because he had no one to care for the perfect land he had created.

In the middle of the creation God placed many trees that would be a source of strength for man, ones he could eat from and receive nourishment. It is here that God placed man for the purpose of working the garden and taking care of it (Gen. 2:15). Along with his job description God gave mankind one command, *"you are free to eat from any tree in the garden; but you must not eat from the tree of the knowledge of good and evil, for when you eat of it you will surely die"* (Gen. 2:16–17).

One thing becomes perfectly clear at this point in the creation narrative: God is the creator. Just because you are a part of his creation does not mean that you can do anything you want to do. Since God was in relationship with his creation, and since he was the creator, he established the boundaries for the relationship and they were simple. He made it clear that Adam could eat of certain trees but one tree was off limits: *the tree of the knowledge of good and evil* (Gen. 2:17).

It is here that we are introduced to two very important realities. First, the fact that something is created "good" did not mean that it was perfect or without the potential for mistake. And secondly, as long as one abides by the guidelines established by God for the relationship, everything will be fine and continue to be good. However, if one chooses to disobey God's rules, they will surely die. This must have been a shock to Adam, especially since he probably had no idea what it meant to die.

That God introduces the matter of dying argues for the idea that, prior to the pronouncement of death, man would live forever. In this sense, he was a candidate for immortality (nondying) and would only live forever if he never disobeyed God's command. It seems likely that this was a potential benefit of God's creation until sin entered into the picture.

In chapter three of Genesis we meet the serpent as he disguises himself as one of the garden animals. He comes to the woman who was created from Adam's rib to be his helper and presents what might best be called the *"great lie."* The serpent tempted Adam and Eve with the idea that God was hiding something from them, namely the possibility of being like him. Unknown to them was that the serpent was an evil foe of God and intent on hurting God and God's creation. According the Scriptures, *"The Great Dragon...that ancient serpent called the devil, or Satan, who leads the whole world astray. He was hurled to earth and his angels with him"* (Rev. 12:9). Satan, the Serpent, was now busy attempting to lead astray God's greatest creation, mankind.

It is interesting to note that the lie of Satan was the exact opposite of God's words. God said *"you will surely die"* (Gen. 2:17) and the serpent said, *"You will not surely die* (Gen. 3:4). Adam and Eve had a choice to make and they made it. Eve succumbed to the pressure of the serpent and encouraged her husband to do the same (Gen. 3:6). Together, they entered uncharted territory in the relationship they shared with God.

An amazing thing happened the moment the couple sinned. Their eyes were opened and they realized that they were naked (Gen. 3:7), which caused them to find a way to cover up. Fortunately, there were plenty of trees in the Garden with ample leaves to cover their nakedness. However, being naked was the least of their problems. They immediately realized that something had happened in their minds and their hearts in terms of their relationship with God. Instead of looking for opportunities to be in fellowship with their creator, they hid (Gen. 3:10).

3

The Other Tree

"Following the path of least resistance is what makes people and rivers crooked!"

—Anonymous

It didn't take long for Adam and Eve to realize the consequences of their sin. Things would not be the same. Even the Serpent would not escape the wrath of God's judgment.

Eve would never be allowed to forget the decision she made that day, for in the pain of childbirth she would be reminded of her fateful choice (1 Tim. 2:15). Adam, ruler over all the land and given the privilege of tending it, would now find the earth he came from most resistant to his work (Gen. 3:17–19). In the end Adam and Eve would live this way until their lives were over and then they would return to the ground, *"since from it you were taken; for dust you are and to dust you will return"* (Gen. 3:19).

THE OTHER TREE

While Adam and Eve were punished for their involvement with the tree of the knowledge of good and evil, there was another tree of special significance in the garden. The tree of life represented something that Adam and Eve had from the beginning: life. Notice in Genesis 2:16 that God does not restrict Adam from eating of the tree of life, only from the tree of the knowledge of good and evil. I have often wondered why the tree of life was not more a part of the conversation between God and the first couple. Only now does it seem to make sense.

There was no reason to restrict Adam from eating from a tree that represented something he already possessed. It was only when Adam had lost the privilege of a potential eternal life that God intervened and made sure that Adam did not eat of this tree. Prior to the couple's sin, Adam and Eve ate from any tree in the garden including the tree of life. The only tree that was off limits before their sin was the tree of the knowledge of good and evil.

God's creation plan included the possibility of mankind living in a perfect relationship with him for eternity. The tree of life provided the possibility of Adam and Eve living forever in their sin, a condition God was determined to prevent. Now, that Adam had wisdom and knowledge it was not out of the question that he would seek to find a way to get to the tree of life, eat of it, and live forever. In God's plan, this could never be allowed to happen.

In Genesis 3:22 we are allowed to listen in on one of the most profound conversations in all of history. Here, we hear the triune God (Father, Son, and Holy Spirit) discuss what they will do with their fallen creation due to the sin in their lives. Their conclusion is swift and clear: Adam and Eve must not be allowed to eat of the tree of life and *live forever in their sin*. That God decided to prohibit Adam and Eve from eating of the tree of life is sufficient proof to argue that man would not live forever in his sinful condition but die as God had determined.

If man was going to live forever the question must be asked, "Why would God go to such extremes to keep Adam and Eve from the garden (tree of life) in order for him not to do that which he was already going to do (live forever)?" Adam was not going to live forever and based on the evidence in Genesis he did not like what God was telling him. It even appears that he resisted God's decision to expel him from the garden (Gen. 3:23).

The words used in the book of Genesis for the action taken by God at this point are undisputed in meaning. God literally drove Adam and Eve out of the garden and gave them a new responsibility. Instead of taking care of the garden, Adam would have to labor hard to work the ground from which he had been taken.

Once Adam and Eve were out of the garden, on the east side, God placed a flaming sword that prevented Adam and Eve from coming back into the garden and making their way to the tree of life. I suspect that for the first time Adam and Eve realized how desperately they needed God. Since they could not make their way to the tree of life, Adam and Eve would have to "work" for a living, raise a family and somehow find their way back to God. Unfortunately, sin had not only brought death to Adam and Eve but a life removed from God. Only God could bring them back. Fortunately, God had not given up on his creation.

4

Good Dirt—Bad Dirt

"The soundest reasoning leads to the wrongest conclusions when the premises are false."

—Vilhjalmur Stefansson

For those who believe that man is naturally immortal (will live forever and not die), the Bible presents a big problem. It might be comforting or troubling to think that man lives his life, dies, and then goes on to heaven or hell, but is that what the Scriptures teach?

God himself contradicts such a belief by the way he treats his greatest creation, mankind. After banishing Adam and Eve from the Garden of Eden due to their sin God defines their destiny in simple terms. Since Adam and Eve were made from the ground, to the ground they would return (Gen. 3:19). If this is not so then we must rethink the creditability of Satan's statement, "you will not surely die" (Gen. 3:4).

I find it interesting that David, a shepherd boy and a king, understood the basic nature of man while so many today miss it completely. David knew that mankind was under a "life" constraint when it comes to praising God (Ps. 146:3–4). For David, once life was over, life was over. Man will not continue to praise God for *"when their spirit departs, they return to the ground; on that very day their plans come to nothing"* (Ps. 146:3–4). On the day of Adam's death he would return to the ground, but what does that mean?

One would certainly think that God knew what was going to happen to man at his death. On the other hand one would not think that God had something else planned for man but decided to tell him that he would return to the ground instead? And besides, man was an intelligent being especially since eating from the tree of the knowledge of good and evil. It seems reasonable to think that Adam and Eve would have argued for a different ending if that was his real nature and if he was wrong that God would set him straight.

The creation of man took place on the sixth day in God's creative agenda. Up to this point, everything that God created was considered good (Gen. 1:31). To be good meant that God was pleased with the outcome. The trees were good, the animals were good, and man was good. It would be unlikely that God would carry out his greatest accomplishment and design it to be incomplete. The truth is that Adam wasn't incomplete just nonliving or in a state of "deadness." God completed man's creation by breathing "into his nostrils the breath of life" (Gen. 2:7).

The idea that man was brought to life by the breath of life suggests that prior to this man was in a state of "deadness" (inactivity) and without life. In other words, he was dirt. According to the Bible, he was good dirt (Gen. 1:31). And even as good dirt, he could not think, feel, or take action on his own. There was nothing inherent in man's nature to make him alive. His condition prior to God bringing him to life is the same condition in which man will exist when he dies and returns to the ground at the end of his life. For Adam, and all of us, to be dead means to be without the life giving spirit of God that makes dead things live.

In what may sound simplistic, man's condition prior to God breathing into him the breath of life is somewhat like a fan without electricity. If the fan is not plugged in. it remains a fan. But, plug the fan into an electric outlet and the fan begins to do what fans do. In a similar way, man was made from the ground but was not "plugged" into his source of power. However, once God breathed the breath of life into man he began to do what God had created him to do. When man dies, the breath of life is taken away and he returns to his original condition prior to being made alive (plugged in).

That Adam is described as becoming a living being or soul (Hebrew *nephesh*) strongly suggests that Adam's prelife condition was the state of the nonliving—the very condition that he will return to once he comes to the end of his life. The truth is that man is *mortal* (will die) and finds his *life only in God* while God alone is *immortal* (1 Tim. 6:16) and never dies. Apart from being plugged in to the source of life, God's breath of life, man will not and cannot exist on his own.

5

Truth and Consequences

"We arrive at truth not by reason alone, but also by the heart"

—Blaine Pascal

Following their expulsion from the garden, Adam and Eve experienced a whole new world. Their daily routine was no longer one of leisure and enjoyment. Life demanded hard work as they faced a world damaged by sin.

The greatest evidence that things had changed for the first couple became clear when Adam died (Gen. 5:5). There's nothing like facing your own mortality that will wake you up to the important matters in life. I can only imagine the conversation that might have taken place between Adam and Eve just before he died. Perhaps it went something like this: "Eve, let this be a reminder to you and our family that what God said is true. Because of man's sin, life will not go on forever, but each one *will* die."

There are many that scoff at such an idea stating that man didn't really die the day God declared it so. However, one must remember that God was not carrying out an execution when he made this promise but making clear the end result should man decide to disobey. The mere evidence that the words *"and then he died"* appear eight times in chapter five of Genesis with reference to the significant men of the line of Adam describes the difference between people inside the garden and those outside. Those outside of the garden die. Even more significant is that these eight men represent the many people who died throughout the time between Adam and Noah. The reality is that countless others experienced the judgment of God upon Adam for his sin that they too would *"surely die"* (Gen. 2:17).

Adam and Eve not only realized that life was not going to go on forever, but that life was different without God. According to the Scriptures, life outside of the garden had taken a downward direction resulting in the first murder (Gen. 4:1–8), finding the hearts of men turning toward evil (Gen. 6:5), and seeing the relationship between God and man becoming so bad that God grieved over having created anything (Gen. 6:6).

God's disappointment with his creation led to the destruction of mankind. Since man was mortal (he would die), God had a decision to make regarding how long he would put up with the evil behavior of his creation. God's decision resulted in the destruction of mankind and all that he had created save the earth. "*Every living thing that moved on the earth perished—birds, livestock, wild animals, all the creatures that swarm over the earth, and all mankind. Everything on dry land that had the breath of life in its nostrils died. Every living thing on the face of the earth was wiped out; men and animals and the creatures that move along the ground were wiped from the earth*" (Gen. 7:21–22). Every creature that had the *breath of life* was destroyed, even mankind. Nevertheless, God was determined to continue man's opportunity to experience life. Perhaps this was because man was the only one made in his *image* (Gen. 1:26).

That God made the decision to destroy mankind and his creation for their sin speaks loudly to the matter of man's nature. If man were immortal, God could not destroy or cause him to perish. If man were immortal, certainly one would expect that the Scriptures would make it clear that what God destroyed would move on to a better place or condition upon their death or destruction. God was starting over and to accomplish this he used the faithfulness of a man named Noah (Gen. 6:8; 6:22).

Noah represented for mankind the only way one could escape the punishment caused by sin. Unlike Cain, who was advised by God to be very careful to do what was right rather than choose evil when sin was at his door, Noah found favor with God through living by faith (Heb. 11:7) and doing what was right (Gen. 6:8, 22).

WHOEVER BELIEVES

It is one thing to rescue righteous people from a worldwide flood but quite another thing to save people from their sins and heal them from a broken relationship with their creator. Only God could do such things. Clearly, this is the intent of John's words in the most famous verse in the entire Bible: John 3:16. Here, John declares that God loves his world and was willing to do anything to save it. Unfortunately, there was no one righteous (Rom. 3:10), not even one who could step in and mend the rift between God and man. This is why God gave his only Son to the world to save it (John 3:17) and not condemn it. This was the only way God could keep his covenant with Noah and Abram and prevent another destruction of mankind. Anyone who believed would not *perish* but receive *eternal life*.

Paul puts it this way. If one lives in sin and never believes in Christ for the forgiveness of his sins, the result is *death: spiritual and physical* (Rom. 6:23). But, if you believe, you will receive *eternal life* as a gift. The reason it is a gift is because it is something that man does not naturally have and can only receive from the one who has the gift. We do not have this gift naturally but it is given to those who believe in Christ who has *"brought life and immortality to light through the gospel"* (2 Tim. 1:10).

According to the New Testament, Christ alone gives immortality, which is the fully realized gift of eternal life to a person when he or she accepts by faith what Christ has done on their behalf through the cross. But given that the original sin of Adam and Eve has destined each person to die and after that to face the judgment (Heb. 9:27), one might ask, "When do we receive immortality?" If not now, how long do we have to wait and what happens until we receive it? If we die before we receive it, what happens when we die?

6

Dead Men Talking

"Before God can deliver us from ourselves, we must undeceive ourselves."

—Augustine

Ever since Adam and Eve received the sentence of death, countless people have died. In other words, each person returned to the condition held by Adam prior to God bringing him to life by breathing the breath of life into his nostrils.

When someone dies that person ceases to be a living being. They are dead. The breath of life (Gen. 7:22) that brought life to their being, returns to God and the nonliving person returns to dust (Gen. 3:19). The occurrence of death is referred to in the Bible by the use of a variety of terms. As previously mentioned, when people died the text in most cases says that he or she died. As we progress through the Old Testament, people are more and more often (thirty-six times) referred to at the end of their lives to have, *"rested [Hebrew Shakhabh] with their fathers"* (2 Kings 8:24; 2 Chron. 33:20). In Psalms 7:5, David describes death in this way: *"then let my enemy pursue and overtake me, let him trample my life to the ground and make me sleep in the dust, Selah."* Or as the psalmist writes in Psalm 13:3, *"Look on me and answer me, O Lord my God. Give light to my eyes, or I will sleep in death."* And Job declares, *"So man lies down and does not, till the heavens are no more, men will not awake or be roused from their sleep"* (Job 14:12).

It is quite clear from the Old Testament texts mentioned above that death was viewed as a time when people rested from their labors, slept in the ground or dust, and awaited the time when they would be aroused. Because we are talking about the use of the analogy of sleeping in an attempt to understand what happens once a person dies, at the risk of oversimplification, let's think for a minute about the matter of sleeping.

The more I think about it, the more I am inclined to believe that sleeping is a perfect way of looking at death. When a person sleeps, time is irrelevant. The next thing a person knows once they fall asleep is that they are waking up in the morning. That a person wakes up is usually attributed to an alarm, a noise, light entering into the room, or that they are completely rested. While each person's experience of sleeping varies to one degree or another, common ground can be found in the idea that during sleep a person knows nothing and is not consciously participating in life.

Jesus himself caught his disciples off guard with the use of this term (fallen asleep) to describe what turns out to be the death of his best friend Lazarus. The disciples, hearing that Lazarus was sleeping (John 11:11–14), were convinced that he would wake up. In their minds there was no need to worry. However, Jesus soon reveals to them that Lazarus was dead (John 11:14). The disciples were confused as to why Jesus waited so long to go and help Lazarus. The sisters of Lazarus, Martha and Mary, also hoped that Jesus would have arrived sooner to prevent the death of their brother (John 11:21, 32). In their way of thinking, Lazarus was dead and it was too late. There's nothing in this text to suggest that Mary and Martha thought that Lazarus had gone on to a better place. When Jesus began to make his move toward the grave of Lazarus in order to raise him from the dead, Mary stated, *"by this time there is a bad odor, for he has been there four days"* (John 11:39).

This is one of the most amazing experiences in the life of Jesus, especially as it relates to our proper understanding of death. Mary reveals that she understood death from a purely physical standpoint. Her brother had been dead for four days and she knew that the process of decay had already begun. Amazingly, David the Psalmist put his faith in God the one who would not allow his body to experience eternal decay in the grave but raise him up in the last day based on what he would do in the future through his Holy One (Ps. 16:10).

The raising of Lazarus from the dead is not only one of the most incredible miracles performed by Christ while on Earth, but the event is equally significant when it comes to developing a theology of the afterlife. I realize that this is not the reason Christ raised Lazarus from the dead but instead so that people would believe that God the Father had sent Jesus to represent him before the world (John 11:42). Nevertheless, some amazing insights can be gained from this event to aid us in our understanding of death.

The first thing we learn about death in this text is that death is physical. Lazarus died from some kind of sickness and his body could no longer survive. He died and, as his sister feared, the process of decay had already begun. Secondly, the idea that someone could have power, even over death, was a concept that was foreign to Mary, Martha, and the other believers. But, most importantly, it's what we *don't* hear that is most interesting.

Think for a minute. Lazarus has been dead for four days and in the minds of many people today this would mean that he is in paradise/heaven, free from his worries and healed from his sickness. However, and without any warning, Lazarus is summoned to return to life and not only live again but die too![1] I am compelled to ask, "Is this the act of a loving God?" Would God bring Lazarus back from paradise/heaven only to have him die again, even if his sisters and Jesus would love to see him one more time? And even more than this, what kind of paradise or heaven can it be without Christ? How can Christ be with the Father and Lazarus in heaven while he is still on Earth? How can Lazarus be in heaven when the Bible reveals (John 14:1–4) that Christ would not prepare a place for all who believe until he dies, is raised from the dead and returns to the Father?

It may sound good to say that Lazarus was already in paradise or heaven but the truth is that he was in the grave awaiting the resurrection of the body to be carried out when Christ returns to Earth (1 Cor. 15). Had Christ not come to his grave that day, Lazarus would have rested with his fathers, remained asleep, and waited to hear the trumpet sound.

Finally, and without question the most surprising and perplexing aspect of this biblical account is the absence of joy and amazement expressed by Lazarus over his encounter with the "other side." Does it not seem strange to you that after the disciples had been sent out two by two that they returned with utter astonishment and joy at how people responded to their ministry and the things they were able to do under the power and influence of the Holy Spirit,[2] but in this case where Lazarus has just returned from paradise not a word is uttered in the text about how great it is and no questions were being asked like, "Why can't I go back?" or "Why did you bring me back to this life when I was experiencing the joy of heaven?"

The reason for the silence is clear and obvious to one who seeks the truth. Lazarus was in the grave, not in paradise. There was nothing to talk about since "*the grave cannot praise you (God), those who go down to the pit cannot hope for your faithfulness. The living, the living—they praise you*" (Isa. 38:18–19) and "*the living know that they will die, but the dead know nothing; they have no further reward, and even the memory of them is forgotten. Their love, their hate and their jealousy have long since vanished; never again will they have a part in anything that happens under the sun*" (Eccles. 9:5). Solomon wrote these words to advise his listeners of the importance of living their life with purpose since, "*Where [they] are going, there is neither working nor planning nor knowledge nor wisdom*" (Eccles. 9:10).

There is however coming a day when all that lay in the graves will come forth. In 1 Corinthians 15, the apostle Paul expounds on that glorious day when Christ will return, raise the dead, and establish his church in victory. And yet the people of the early church wondered about the fate of those who were beginning to die all the while continuing to believe in a second coming of Christ their Lord (1 Thess. 4:13–18). In view of this, one is compelled to ask, "If the dead were in fact not dead but in paradise, what justifiable reason would there be for the second coming?" Paul describes the second coming as a mystery (1 Cor. 15:51), so perhaps this is the reason he needed to explain it to the believers of his day and present an argument for why we must hear it in ours, too.

7

Friend or Foe?

"Some secrets are worth keeping. Others are too good to keep!"

—Anonymous

The Greek word mystery (Grk. *musterion*) is an appropriate term to describe the feelings people of the first century had concerning the dissonance between the message about the soon return of Christ and the daily happenings in their lives. All the talk about Jesus coming again was making many Christians uneasy—especially those in Thessalonica since some of their friends and family had started to die (1 Thess. 4:13–18).

The reality of death was nothing new, but the idea that you could live beyond the grave—at some point in the future because you believed in Christ—was. What, however, was one to think when the promise of eternal life gave way to death and grief? No one was more baffled over this than the Christians in Thessalonica. Eventually, their confusion led them to seek answers from the apostle Paul.

Paul sought to alleviate the ignorance of the believers over the perceived ambiguity of his message (1 Thess. 4:13–18) by explaining to them how their faith gave them hope in the face of death instead of being left to grieve like the rest of the world. The suggestion that people without Christ have no hope against the grave (1 Thess. 4:13) argues strongly for the idea that death was seen as the end and not a passage way to a better life.

What then could a believer in the first century expect concerning the mysterious nature of death? According to the Lord's own words, death would hold its grip on mankind until the second coming at which time the *"dead in Christ will rise first"* (1 Thess. 4:16). Throughout Paul's response it is impossible not to see the centrality of the resurrection when it comes to understanding what happens when a person dies.

17

According to Christ, those who are dead will rise first at the time of the resurrection. Along with the Christians who are still alive, those who have died will meet Christ in the air. This message was at the heart of the gospel (Grk. *euaggelion*) and was intended to be an encouragement to those who were confused about the death of their family and friends.

AT THE SOUNDING OF THE TRUMPET

When Paul speaks about the resurrection in the New Testament he mentions the sound of the trumpet, a sound intended to wake up those who have fallen asleep. If man is only spiritual in nature—as many will seek to propose—why must the Bible insist on the importance of the second coming and the resurrection?

No one argued more strongly for the centrality of the resurrection than the apostle Paul. 1 Corinthians 15 provides an excellent overview of resurrection day and why it is fundamental to the future of the believer. Apparently, there were some in Paul's time that failed to see the significance of the resurrection going so far as to deny its probability (1 Cor. 15:12).

WHAT IF?

The presence of false teaching regarding the resurrection prompted Paul to make it clear that our resurrection is actually dependent on the resurrection of Christ. If Christ has not been resurrected, then those who have "fallen asleep" (died) are lost.

The idea of the dead being lost is somewhat of a misnomer. In this case, being lost carries less of the idea of being hard to find but rather the sense of irretrievable. If Christ has not been raised from the dead, those who have died are hopelessly lost and can not be brought back. For them, it's over.

But Paul states that this is not the case. Christ has been raised from the dead and referred to by Paul as "*the firstfruits*" (1 Cor. 15:20). This is an extremely significant term for Paul in referring to Christ's role in the resurrection. Since Christ is the firstfruits of those who have fallen asleep, he is the first to be resurrected or come out of death victoriously. Anyone else who has been raised from the dead is destined to die again (Lazarus). In addition to these are those who have been spared physical death (Enoch, Elijah). Having not gone through death, these saints of old do not factor into Paul's teaching. According to Paul, Christ is not only the firstfruits of death, he is the only one who has claimed victory over the great enemy and provides the hope of life beyond the grave at the time of the resurrection for those who believe in Him. Being the firstfruits he promises a great harvest of resurrected people at the second coming.

Our time to be resurrected however will come according to Paul. Just as all die in Adam (1 Cor. 15:22), all who believe and are in Christ *"will be made alive"* (1 Cor. 15:22). Interestingly, we find in this text that Paul gives us the sequence for this event. First, Christ will be raised, *"then, when he comes, those who belong to him"* (1 Cor. 15:23). Paul puts to rest the idea that people can be raised or pass on to a different life before Christ the firstfruits has given us the final victory over our enemy known as death.

One might wonder about the millions of people who have lived prior to the initial coming of Christ: his life, death, and resurrection. Is it possible for people to enter a life beyond the grave even before Christ has come to the earth? Again, I must ask, "What kind of 'heaven' or 'kingdom' can there be without Christ?"

Even though Christ has become the firstfruits over death, death itself will not be dealt its final blow until the resurrection for the last enemy to go is death itself (1 Cor. 15:26). Surprisingly many people today do not look at death in this way.

A DIFFERENT VIEW

Go to any funeral today and you will hear that death is an entrance to a different life. In many cases it seems not to matter whether or not the person is a believer. I have attended many services where the pastor has described death in these "rosy" terms, *almost as if it is a friend.*

Despite the fact that people are sad and upset about the death of their loved one, they still believe that the person is better off and walking the streets of heaven. Why then, I must ask, did Jesus cry at the graveside of Lazarus even though he knew that he was about to raise him from the dead? Couldn't he have simply said to Mary, Martha, and the disciples that they shouldn't worry because he was going to raise him out of the grave? Better yet, would Jesus put on fake tears just to make everyone feel better? Or, is it more likely that Jesus understood the pain of the family and knew how helpless they were in the face of this enemy we call death? Could it be that Jesus knew that death would claim many more lives in the future due to the sin of mankind and that final victory over this enemy would not take place until the resurrection? Without question, he knew.

BODY LIFE

If death is not a doorway to another life, then what happens when we die? What kind of existence can we expect to have before and when Christ returns?

According to the book of Genesis, God created mankind out of the dust of the earth. God's greatest creation was perfectly fit for living on earth (1 Cor. 15:38). At the time of the resurrection, God will give man another body. It will no longer be a purely physical body, but a "heavenly" body fit for the kingdom (1 Cor. 15:40). Paul describes it this way: *"The body that is sown perishable, it is raised imperishable; it is sown in dishonor, it is raised in glory; it is sown in weakness, it is raised in power; it is sown a natural body, it is raised a spiritual body"* (1 Cor. 15:42–44).

The pattern for what will take place at the resurrection has been set by Adam and Christ. Through Adam we all entered this world as dust and to dust we will return at death (Gen. 3:19). In Christ we will all enter the kingdom of God with spiritual bodies like his. No longer will we have the limitations of the flesh but in a twinkling of an eye, at the sounding of the trumpet, we will all be changed to have bodies fit for the kingdom. Most significantly, we will all be changed from mortal into immortal beings (1 Cor. 15:53). What was lost in the garden due to sin will be reinstated in the kingdom because of faith in Christ. Until then, we wait and we rest until we hear those final words: *"Death has been swallowed up in victory…. Where, O death, is your victory? Where, O death, is your sting?…But thanks be to God! He gives us the victory through our Lord Jesus Christ"* (1 Cor. 15:54–57).

8

Dead Silence

"It's not really that hard to stop sinning all at once. All you have to do is die!"

—Anonymous

Death is a puzzling episode in the course of life. It is an occurrence that everyone must experience (Heb. 9:27), yet one that prohibits a great deal of evaluation. Very few people having died have ever returned with hard empirical evidence about the nature of death.

Some who have professed having an "out of the body" experience fail to provide sufficient information concerning death that would lead one to think that they have actually encountered life beyond the grave. It's going to take a great deal more than "I saw a bright light" to serve as convincing proof for belief in an immediate life beyond the grave.

In the Bible we read about people who were brought back to life after dying. In two of the passages, the person raised from the dead was described in terms of being "asleep," a term used throughout the Bible for the experience of death. At no time during these events did the one who was raised from the dead declare, "You can't believe what it was like to be dead!" In one passage (Mark 5:43), after Jesus raised the little girl from the dead, he instructed the family to get her something to eat. This is somewhat of a surprising order if the girl had entered the kingdom of God and was sharing in the bounty of God's resources during her time of death. On the other hand it seems quite appropriate if she had not eaten. The Bible declares that there will be no planning, working, knowledge, or wisdom needed in death (Eccles. 9:10). Therefore, it seems safe to assume that eating will not be taking place in death as well. Rejoicing and feasting, while both are a vital part of life, are not a part of the grave but delayed until the time of the resurrection. The idea of eating in the kingdom was mentioned by Jesus to his disciples on the last night of his earthly life. Referring to the Passover, Jesus told his disciples that he would not "eat it again until it finds fulfillment in the kingdom

21

of God" (Luke 22:16). If Jesus was not to eat the Passover until he established his future kingdom, there is no way that he was there to eat with the little girl he raised from the dead. Again, I must ask, "What kind of kingdom banquet would it be without the guest of honor?" In this case Jesus gave the order to feed the little girl only because she was once again part of the living.

DEAD SILENCE

Lazarus was a good friend of Jesus and one would think quite comfortable around his Lord. Because of this, it is hard to think that he would be quiet about his experience in the grave. His sisters, Martha and Mary, were not shy about telling Jesus that if He had been there sooner their brother would not have died (John 11:21, 32).

It is easy to forget that Lazarus was not only a friend of Jesus, but Jesus was his Lord. Can you imagine living in the first century, convinced that you had found the Messiah, but discovering that you were sick unto death? I would expect Lazarus to hope that Jesus would come and heal him. Lazarus may have hoped for this but his experience was different. He died. From our perspective, the next thing Lazarus knew is that he was walking out of the grave with a cloth around him and hearing Jesus say, *"Take off the grave clothes and let him go"* (John 11:44).

Now I'm not a psychologist or psychiatrist professing to understand completely the way people think and act but I'm fairly confident of one thing. If Lazarus had been to heaven, one would think he would have said something about this glorious place. If the crippled man healed by Peter and John in Acts 3:1–8 went through the streets *"walking, jumping and praising God"* as a result of his miracle, don't you think Lazarus would have demonstrated some excitement over seeing *"what God has prepared for those who love him"* (1 Cor. 2:9). However, the Scripture is absolutely silent when it comes to recording the words of Lazarus regarding his experience in the grave. Instead, what we find is evidence that Lazarus was giving testimony that Jesus had indeed raised him from the "dead," not stories about what Lazarus found on the other side. A few days after Lazarus' resurrection, he is found lying at the table of our Lord endorsing the way Mary was worshipping at the feet of Jesus (John 12:2). Lazarus' testimony to the power of God was so strong that the chief priests sought to kill him, too (John 12:9–10)!

Interestingly, the Bible declares that the dead are silent (Ps. 115:17) and that there is no praise or love of God declared in the grave (Ps. 88:11–12). It stands to reason that if this is true it's because the person who is dead does not know what's going on (Eccles. 9:5–6), or otherwise he would shout it to the hilltops. Lazarus was silent in the grave and silent in his second opportunity for life not because he didn't want to say anything but because he didn't have anything to say.

Lazarus is a member of a long list of people who have trusted God with their lives and trusted Him even in their death. The writer to the Hebrews (Heb. 11) describes these men and women as people of faith. His list, while extensive, has at least a few common threads running throughout its membership. First, each man or woman is different in how they served God. Secondly, each one was able to please God by faith alone. And, finally each person of faith is still waiting for his or her reward (Heb. 11:39).

Each person received the hand of God's blessing while they were living their life of faith yet none of them received their final reward (Heb. 11:39). According to the writer of Hebrews, *"God had planned something better for us so that only together with us would they be made perfect"* (Heb. 11:40). Years ago we used to tell a joke about Grant's tomb. It went like this: "Do you know who's buried in Grant's tomb?" The person would usually say something silly like, "No, who?" And we would reply, "Grant, of course!" I am tempted to ask you, "Do you know who's buried in Abraham, Isaac, and Jacob's tomb?" But, of course you know the answer: Abraham, Isaac, and Jacob.

The conclusion is simple. These men and women are buried in their tombs because they are dead and they have not heard the call of the trumpet. God is waiting until that final day when, along with you and me, he will call them out of the grave. Nevertheless, these men and women continue to speak to us even though they are dead (Heb. 11:4).

9

Join the Club!

"He who marries the spirit of this age will soon find himself a widower."

—William R. Inge

A few years ago a lady attending a seniors' aerobics class in our church offered me a kitten. The idea of having a kitten was a new one for me since I was raised only having a dog but most importantly my wife was a little skittish on the thought. I thought I had avoided the temptation until the lady brought the kitten to the church one day. One look was all it took.

That beautiful kitten became our "Magic" and before long we had kittens to boot! Now, four years later I clearly understand the saying that "curiosity killed the cat." Our cats are curious about everything, especially bags. One cannot get through emptying the groceries without Magic or one her kittens getting inside a bag. One thing I've learned watching this feline phenomenon is certain. While curiosity can provide some exciting adventures, it rarely answers all of your questions.

The truth is cats are not the only ones who are curious about life. Human beings have searched for answers to life's most perplexing questions for years too, a practice not expected to end anytime soon. Death, too, has been a matter of great interest for people throughout history. What could one expect? Is death the end, and if not, will man live again and under what conditions?

Wondering what death brings was a question on the minds of many of the first century Christians. The fact that family members were dying brought great concern for those who believed strongly in the apostle Paul's teaching on the second coming of Christ and a hope beyond the grave (1 Thess. 4:13–18). The reality of man's mortality began to bring into clear focus the question of whether or not man would cease to exist beyond the grave. In other words, is death really the end?

DEAD OR ALIVE

For many, to be dead is a kind of spiritual oxymoron for to be dead is really to be alive. In this sense, death is no longer considered to be death but a passage way into a new realm or experience for the believer. This, however, would appear to violate the heart of the apostle Paul's teaching concerning the resurrection (1 Cor. 15). If people immediately enter another life (eternal life) beyond the grave, the resurrection is unnecessary.

One only needs to read a few verses in Paul's writings to the Christians in Thessalonica to discover that there was a real problem over the fact that people were dying before Christ returned. One can understand their confusion since they expected Christ to return before anyone died. In an attempt to satisfy their curiosity Paul spoke of the resurrection. How this would help can only be determined by taking a closer look at Paul's view on this life-changing event.

HIS RESURRECTION AND OURS

The resurrection was more than a new teaching. For Paul, it was at the heart of the gospel message (1 Cor. 15:3–8; (Grk. *euaggelion*), and something that sealed the truth of Christ into his heart. It was one thing to preach about the life of Christ and another to proclaim his power to change a life, but even more significant to see the risen Lord yourself and know that he is master over man's greatest enemy, death. The task Paul now faced was simple; could he convince those who sought him out for answers?

ASLEEP, NOW WHAT?

Dying was nothing new to the Christians of the first century but dying knowing Christ as Lord, was. Paul's first challenge was to show the believers that the death, burial, and resurrection of Christ were critical to the future resurrection of mankind. If Christ himself had not been raised from the dead everyone was found to be hopeless (1 Cor. 15:12–19). Having been one of the fortunate ones to see Christ after his resurrection, Paul affirms that Christ has indeed been raised from the dead (1 Cor. 15:8, 20).

Christ is called the "firstfruits" of those who have fallen asleep or died. Just as Adam brought death to mankind, Christ would bring life to humanity by overcoming its greatest foe: death. Years ago, I use to read about how farmers would speak of the firstfruits of the crop they expected to bring in. By taking a good look at the firstfruits the farmer was able to determine what kind of crop he might reap down the road. By taking a look at Christ we are able to determine the kind of fruit we might bear in the end.

Paul makes it clear that there is an order to this spiritual harvest. First, Christ would rise from the dead (firstfruits) and then when he comes, those who belong to him (1 Cor. 15:23). Notice that Paul not only gives us the order but the time and place. While Christ has already achieved victory over death by rising from the dead, believers will not share in this victory until the second coming. It is at this time that Christ will have his ultimate victory: a time when death will be destroyed for good (1 Cor. 15:26).

I'LL BE BACK

The twentieth-century movie industry featured many wonderful actors and perhaps none more prominent than Arnold Schwarzenegger, known to many as the *Terminator*. Throughout Arnold's career, he has become known for the phrase: "I'll be back!" Throughout the teaching of the apostle Paul concerning the future work of Christ, the Lord Jesus was also known for the same phrase: "I'll be back!" He promised that he would return to complete the work he started when he came out of the grave.

THE TESTIMONY OF JOHN

John, the beloved disciple, is one of the most important testimonies to the promises of Christ. His writings in the gospel of John reveal an understanding of Christ not seen in any other part of the New Testament. He was called the beloved disciple because he was very close to Christ. While Christ had his inner circle of Peter, James, and John, John was even closer. Certainly he would have known what Christ had said concerning his plans for the future even if he didn't understand it all.

While it is true that some parts of the end-time teaching found in the New Testament are unclear, John's writings concerning the second coming of Christ are not. After telling his disciples that he would be going away and that they could not go where he was going, Jesus promised to return and get them (John 14:1–4).

The purpose of his return was to get the believers he had left behind so that they could be with him again. This is the way he put it: "*And if I go and prepare a place for you, I will come back and take you to be with me that you also may be where*

I am" (John 14:4). After reading this text, one is prompted to ask a simple question: "If people are immortal beings that continue to live beyond death why would Christ need to return to get them so they can be with him and be where he is?" The only way this verse makes sense is if Christ is not with them following death because they are in the grave and are awaiting the resurrection.

JOIN THE CLUB

Those who have recently died and are awaiting the resurrection of believers are in good company with saints who have died before. Men and women of old who now line what has been called the hall of faith mentioned in the book of Hebrews lay in waiting for the second coming of Christ. The writer to the Hebrews declares that these people were commended for their faith and that the world was not worthy of them (Heb. 11:38–39). Nevertheless, in the end they did not receive what had been promised—a better resurrection (Heb. 11:35), for *"God had promised something better for us so that only together with us would they be made perfect"* (Heb. 11:40).

Just think about it. People like David, Samson, Abraham, Isaac, Moses, Joseph, and everyone else are awaiting the day when Christ will order the sounding of the trumpet that will call all men out of the grave to meet him in the air (1 Thess. 4:13–18). When it comes to the second coming, no one gets the advantage and what a day that will be.

BODY LANGUAGE

Not only were people curious about the status of those who had fallen asleep but found themselves wondering about the type of bodies they would have when Christ returned (1 Cor. 15:35). One thing's for sure, the bodies would be different than our earthly bodies and fit for the kingdom of God.

One might ask, "What kind of body is fit for the kingdom of God? How exactly will it be different from our physical body?" If the Scripture is written in a way to help us understand this kind of question, then we might take a hint from the risen body of our Lord. Prior to his death and resurrection, Christ ate as any person would for strength and health; afterwards he ate, too (Luke 24:40; John 21:11–14). Before, he walked everywhere he went and did things in a normal and routine manner but afterwards he appeared in places without using a door (John 20:19, 26). Before, one could recognize Christ from his appearance. Afterwards, Christ could conceal his identity from people who knew all about him (Luke

24:13–45). Could it be that this is the kind of body we will have at the second coming of Christ? Whatever the nature of our bodies, it is clear from Paul's writing that it is a body from Christ that is from heaven and not one that comes from the ground (1 Cor. 15:47). His likeness will be our likeness. One minute we will be like Adam and the next we will become like him. In a twinkling of an eye, we will all be changed.

Our bodies won't be made up of flesh and blood for they cannot inherit the kingdom of God (1 Cor. 15:50), nor will they be perishable, dishonorable, weak, natural, or mortal. At the second coming each of these characteristics will change. We will be changed into an imperishable body, one that is clothed in honor, filled with power and immortal. Death no longer will have a grip on those who are in Christ. Only then will the believer find the fulfillment of God's promise to be with him forever (1 Thess. 4:17).

THE BIG CHANGE

More than anything else, believers will be transformed from mortal or dying beings into immortal or nondying beings. Throughout the Bible people are always spoken of as mortal beings rather than immortal. Nowhere in the entire Bible are people spoken of as immortal beings or souls, for God alone is considered immortal (1 Tim. 6:16) and the gift of immortality is always seen as something received or given at the time of the second coming of Christ (1 Cor. 15:54).

Eternal life, a gift given at the time of believing in Christ is the gift of immortality in promise (Rom. 6:23). It is the privilege of knowing Christ personally (John 17:3) and is a promise that by being "in Christ" one will never perish (John 3:16). A person in Christ is never promised that he will not die but that he will not cease to exist in the end. This means that a person cannot live eternally without dying for he is destined to experience the penalty of death first and then face judgment (Heb. 9:27). However, a person can perish when Christ returns if he has not received the gift of eternal life prior to death, which guarantees the transformation of our mortal bodies into an immortal being at the second coming.

From the words of the New Testament, one can read that man seeks after immortality, a gift found only in the life of Jesus Christ (Rom. 2:7); a gift that has been revealed in Christ through the preaching of the gospel (2 Tim. 1:10). It is along the path of life that man lost his potential for immortality and along this same path that he finds his forsaken gift (Gen. 2:17; 3:22; Prov. 12:28), but only at the second coming. What a victory that will be but what is to be said for the man without Christ? Now that's a different story!

10

Perish the Thought!

"Some things have to be believed to be seen!"

—Anonymous

I can clearly remember sitting in the pew of a church years ago and singing a familiar song. The words went like this: "Rescue the perishing, care for the dying." Now, years later, I realize that I was one of the perishing people until I met Christ.

I'm quite certain that at that time I didn't think a great deal about the idea or meaning of perishing. In fact, I may have not even known what it meant. But today, in view of God's teaching on what happens at the second coming, it is important to understand the true meaning of *perish*. One thing it doesn't mean is to *die*. Dying is not perishing, as we are all destined to die and then at some time in the future face the judgment of God (Heb. 9:27), at which time we will receive either the reward or punishment for our life's decision regarding Christ.

The words translated *perish* appear eighty-two times in the Bible. In each occurrence the word suggests the idea of ceasing to exist or to be no more. On a rare occasion the word can be understood to mean the same as die, as in the use of Esther when she comments on her decision to go before the King without being summoned, "*If I perish, I perish*" (Esther 4:16) or in the words of Job as he ponders the question, "*Why did I not perish at birth?*" (Job 3:11). However, the overwhelming intended meaning of the word *perish* is to exist no more.

Man cannot avoid the verdict of death placed upon his life through the decision of Adam (1 Cor. 15:22), but he can receive the gift of immortality, which is his guarantee that he will not perish. According to Peter, God does not want anyone to perish (2 Peter 3:9), a promise already made through John (John 3:16). Notice that Peter does not say *die*. God has already pronounced the verdict of death upon mankind through Adam (Gen. 2:17; 1 Cor. 15:22), yet he wants so much and is even patient to not carry out the order to perish until the last moment (2 Peter 3:9).

Given that God does not want anyone to perish argues strongly for the idea that God will cause people to perish if they do not know him as Lord. Even a cursory reading of the Bible's use of the word *perish* will reveal a clear teaching regarding the intended meaning of the word. David the Psalmist declares that the wicked (spiritually lost) will be like the beauties of the field. They will vanish like smoke (Ps. 37:20) and they will never endure (Ps. 49:12). Job paints an amazing analogy between the idea that man without God will perish, and the impossibility of his own dung surviving (Job 20:7). Given time, the dung will cease to exist. Eventually, people will look for him but never be able to find him. He will perish.

In the gospel of John, Jesus reveals a similar picture of the difference between *dying* and *perishing*. Jesus and the disciples had just arrived in Bethany, the place where Lazarus lived and now had died (John 11). In an attempt to comfort Martha and to reveal to her the truth about life, death, and the resurrection, Jesus makes this statement, *"I am the resurrection and the life. He who believes in me will live, even though he dies; and whoever lives and believes in me will never die. Do you believe this?"* (John 11:25–26).

One thing is perfectly clear about Jesus's statement, namely, that *dying* and *perishing* are not the same. Here, Jesus is referring to the idea that for people who believe in him they will never die even though they die. This may sound like double-talk but given the context in which this statement is being made it makes sense. Due to the juxtaposition of the words *die* and *die* in this text we can see that Jesus is playing one against the other. The text reveals that in the first case *dying* refers to physical death and in the second, death refers to immortality or an undying nature, which means that the person will not *perish* (cease to exist). No one would venture to say that Christ is teaching in this text that no one will ever die for clearly that is not true. On the contrary, Christ is proclaiming that even in the face of death and dying people in Christ can have the hope of not perishing for he is *"the resurrection and the life"* (John 11:25).

What then can be said of those without Christ? When and where will they perish? Part of our consideration regarding these questions must begin with a proper understanding of the place of destruction known as hell. It is in hell that the wicked will find their destruction and cease to exist.

WHERE IN HELL?

There is perhaps no other word more misunderstood in the Bible than the word *hell.* It is particularly difficult to determine the actual meaning of the word without knowing what word is used in the text. Four different words are used throughout the Bible to refer to *hell* (*Sheol, Hades, Gehenna,* and *tartaroo*[1]), which demands that we understand which word is being used in order to accurately determine the meaning of the text.

By examining each occurrence of the word, one will discover that the word *hell* can range in meaning from a place of judgment, the grave or abode of the dead, to a mythological place where rebellious gods were confined. The most common word translated *hell* in the New Testament is the word *Gehenna,* which is referred to as the place of judgment. In every case, Jesus speaks of *Gehenna* with reference to judgment, while *Hades* is seen as referring to the grave or place of the dead. In the only other places where different words are used for *hell* (Luke 16:23; 2 Peter 2:4), one can examine the context and determine that something other than judgment is meant.

GET THE PICTURE?

While it is clear from Jesus's use of the word *hell (Gehenna)* that we are talking about a place of judgment, there are other aspects that can be determined biblically about the nature of *hell,* (Gehenna) that distinguishes it from the *hell,* (hades) that refers to the grave?

The word *Gehenna* is taken from a place in Jerusalem that was named after *"the valley of the son of Ben Hinnom"* (Josh. 15:8) which ran southward from the Jaffa Gate to the west side of the city, then eastward and southward of the city to the valley of Kidron. The valley was used as a dumping or garbage area and at one time was even used for sacrifices made to Molech.[2] In time the Jewish apocalyptic leaders began to call the valley of Hinnom the entrance to hell itself.

It is not surprising then that Jesus used the valley of Hinnom, or the *Gehenna* garbage dump, as an image for the place of punishment known as hell. It was a place of destruction. Garbage was placed here to be burned and destroyed. Images used in the books of Matthew and Revelation which picture hell as a fiery furnace (Matt. 13:42, 50) or a lake of burning sulfur (Rev. 20:10) are not that far off from the image of a place of destruction. John the apostle makes clear that the *"lake of fire"* into which the beast and the false prophet were thrown (Rev. 19:20) is known as the second death (Rev. 20:14b).

The confusion regarding hell comes from those who believe that Gehenna hell is eternal. That is, that the fires of hell continue to go on and on forever without ever coming to an end. The idea of an eternal Gehenna hell going on forever and ever is, in the first place, contrary to the image of a garbage dump that burns long enough to consume the garbage. Where is the garbage dump of Jerusalem now? Is it still burning?

The idea of a hell that burns forever is challenged by the teaching found in the book of Jude (Jude 7) regarding the destruction of Sodom and Gomorrah. Jude writes concerning those who *"gave themselves up to sexual immorality and perversion. They serve as an example of those who suffer the punishment of eternal fire."* In this text we notice the language of suffering and punishment combined with an eternal fire. Nowhere does Jude suggest that the people of Sodom and Gomorrah are still being punished or suffering. Nowhere does he say that the fires are continuing to burn outside the cities. Rather, he presents that the fires continue to burn but only in effect and result.

That something is being described as "eternal" is nothing new to the pages of Scripture. There are many occurrences of this word being used to describe the many realities of life with or without Christ. The most common term, *"eternal life,"* is a gift given to those who believe in Christ (Rom. 6:23); a gift that is given once on the basis of faith. It is not continually given over eternity. In Mark 3:29, those who are guilty of blaspheming against the Holy Spirit are said to have committed an *"eternal sin."* Certainly this was not intended to mean that from that point on the person is continually sinning against the Holy Spirit but rather that the sin has an eternal effect upon the person committing the sin. He will always be guilty of having committed this sin. In the book of Hebrews the writer describes Jesus as the source of *"eternal salvation"* (Heb. 5:9). No one would suggest that a person is continually being saved over and over again. This would clearly speak against a passage like Romans 10:10 which states that a person is "saved" when they confess with their mouth and believe in their heart that Jesus is Lord (Rom. 10:9) instead of being saved continuously.

Other uses of the word eternal (Grk. *aionios*) include the idea of God's *"eternal purpose"* (Eph. 3:11), which he accomplished in Christ Jesus. This is a purpose that has been established before the foundation of the world and will last forever. It is not meant to suggest that God is repeatedly establishing his purpose for mankind. No, God has determined his purpose and it will stand forever.

In Paul's second letter to the Thessalonians (2 Thess. 2:16), the believers are reminded of the *"eternal encouragement and good hope"* which has been given to them by Christ Jesus and God the Father. Through the gift of encouragement from God the believers are exhorted to stand firm in the faith. One would not expect to think that God is encouraging believers every moment, but rather that he is providing a source of encouragement in the Holy Spirit and belief in the truth (2 Thess. 2:13).

The writer to the Hebrew Christians ends his letter praying that God will equip the believers with everything they need to do his good will (Heb. 13:20–21) based on the *"eternal covenant"* that was established through the blood of Christ. Few would think, if any, that God is entering into this covenant again and again to ensure believers are taken care of as they do his will. Of course not! God entered into a lasting or eternal covenant on our behalf. Once the covenant was sealed, its benefit was forever available to those who commit to Christ.

The kingdom (2 Peter 1:11) of our Lord is something for which every believer longs. Therefore, Peter advises each of us to be diligent to make sure of our calling and be absolutely certain that we are "in Christ." Having made sure, we will receive a rich welcome into the *"eternal kingdom"* of our Lord and Savior Jesus Christ. This is not a kingdom that keeps on happening, but one that will never end once entered. You will always be a part of this kingdom. Once you're a member, you're always a member.

As if these were not convincing enough in terms of realizing that eternal has more to do with result than process, let's take a closer look at some of the word combinations found in Scripture that cause a great deal of trouble with respect to the nature of hell. For instance, the writer to the Hebrews apparently likes this word as he uses it in connection with "eternal" salvation, covenant, judgment and inheritance. In terms of judgment the writer to the Hebrews wants to make sure that this matter is one of the core beliefs in the life of the believer. What God determines is final when it comes to the action He takes regarding our faith in Him. One who makes this claim cannot continue to have a lack of faith but prove oneself diligent in his or her walk of faith (Heb. 6:4–12). In regards to *"eternal judgment,"* whatever God decides is final and not open for debate. We are encouraged as believers not to be continually changing our minds about our relationship with God. In some way, this would nullify in our lives the action God takes on our behalf based on the work of Christ.

There is perhaps no other word that demonstrates the intent of the use of the word *eternal* than the word given by the author of Hebrews when he speaks of the work of Christ that has secured for each believer an *"eternal inheritance"* (Heb. 9:15). The idea of an inheritance is clear. Vary rarely is an inheritance given gradually or in increments. When someone receives an inheritance he receives it in full. He may decide to use it in increments or all at once, but the inheritance is given to him in full. When God gives his children an "*eternal inheritance*," it is expected to last a lifetime, for the price or ransom has been paid in full. The believer does not have to continually go back again and again and make draws on the inheritance. He simply has to receive it.

Finally, there is the matter of "*eternal punishment*" (Matt. 25:46) for those who are not found to be true servants of God at the coming of the Son of Man (Matt. 25:31). Each one will appear before the throne of God and be separated to the right or to the left. On the right he will place those who know God and have lived according to His desires. On the left he will group those who may have said that they knew God, but who, in reality, never knew him and never lived according to his desires (Matt. 25:41–45). In the end he will send those on his left to "*eternal punishment*" and those on his right to "*eternal life*" (Matthew 25:46).

The interesting thing about this passage is that when we adopt the idea of everlasting punishment that goes on and never ends, we raise a number of questions that are difficult to answer. For example, if man who is "mortal" (he will die) is to experience everlasting punishment in an eternal fire (Matt. 25:41), how will he survive? Can a man that is mortal eternally exist in a fire that apparently doesn't burn? Would that not mean that he is immortal? If we adopt the idea of an "eternal fire" into which the goats (nonbelievers) are thrown that goes on forever (Matt. 25:41), do we not violate the teaching found in Jude 7 which speaks of a fire that has eternal results rather than an eternal process? And furthermore, Matthew speaks of the process of separating for punishment and reward taking place when the Son of Man comes back and not immediately after death. What then are we to make of the intermediate time between death and the coming of the Son of Man?

It appears that the Scripture speaks for itself and clearly answers these questions. Paul writes in his letter to the Christians in Rome that the wages of sin is death, but the free gift of God is "*eternal life*"[3] (Rom. 6:23). Are we talking about a type of life that keeps on being passed out as a gift to those who believe or is it a one-time gift? And who exactly receives this gift? Even though the person in Matthew 25, who does not know Christ receives a life of eternal punishment, would we not call this eternal life?

CONCLUSIONS

What are we to think? Can a mortal man enter into an eternal fire and live eternally even though he is not immortal? Isn't it the Bible's position that only those in Christ receive the gift of eternal life?

For years people have proposed that this is the Bible's teaching regarding the future of the man who is without Christ yet the evidence presents a different picture of the truth. How one might ask could we have reached such a conclusion? Perhaps no other passage of Scripture has influenced our thinking regarding this subject as the story of the rich man and Lazarus in Luke 16, a story to which we now turn our attention.

11

Hell, What Do I Know?

"You can tell when you're on the right track—it's usually uphill."

—Anonymous

The idea that Luke 16 represents the Bible's best explanation of the nature of hell is commonly accepted around the world. When I am confronted with this teaching, I often make an attempt to share some thoughts concerning the text that might bring this belief into question. Recently, after sharing with a pastor regarding this text, he asked me, "How can I know more about this teaching?" The answer was simple: just study the text. It is my contention that many people believe what they have been told concerning Luke 16 for the simple reason that they have never been challenged to look deeper into the true meaning of this passage. In the following pages I invite you to take a different look at the story told by Jesus and make a decision for yourself.

A DIFFERENT LOOK

As I have stated, the Bible is not that difficult to understand for the most part. While not all passages are equally clear most can be explained after careful exegesis. For this reason alone Luke 16 should be examined and not allowed to mean something that violates its given context yet this appears to be the dilemma. It is certainly worth a second look.

No matter where I go, people are determined to call the story of the rich man and Lazarus a literal story used by Jesus to describe the realities of hell—a conclusion that will not hold up under a closer examination of the text. I find believers who use this as a proof text regarding hell that cannot explain it but even more amazingly I find Christians who don't agree with the idea that Luke 16 is literal who likewise can't show how this text is not intended to describe the specifics of hell. In the following pages, I hope to provide the biblical evidence for such a challenge to this text.

THE AUDIENCE

Jesus was a master at knowing his audience. Every time he spoke, whether it was in front of the masses or before his disciples on a hillside, he always spoke with purpose. His words were spoken in an effort to hit his target. We should not expect anything different in Luke 16. In Luke 16 and in the surrounding chapters, Jesus is speaking to a mixed group of tax collectors, sinners, Pharisees, and teachers of the law (Luke 15:1). Usually, one can determine what people are thinking by the way they respond. In this case the Pharisees and the teachers of the law were found to be grumbling over what Jesus was teaching and doing. Luke writes that they muttered and proclaimed that this man, Jesus, *"welcomes sinners and eats with them"* (Luke 15:2).

THE TACTIC

Not only did Jesus know his audience, but he was willing to speak to their issues. His most common way of doing this was to speak through the telling of parables. By taking a close look at the context, one can see Jesus's tactic being employed once again (Luke 15:7, 8–10, 11–32; 16:1–15, 19–31). For those intent on arguing that Luke 16:19–31 is not a parable, proof that it is not a parable must be shown—a view that does not appear to be supported by the context.

Not only does Jesus speak to the crowd by using parables, but he uses parables that speak to the issue at hand. From these passages one can see that the Pharisees and the teachers of the law were extremely prejudicial toward others, believing that they alone were in a right relationship with God. Knowing of their prejudices, Jesus tells a series of parables about the way God cares about everyone and everything—whether it's a coin, a sheep or a person. God will not rest until the lost are found, even if the lost is a beggar, a tax collector, or a prostitute. Further confirmation that Jesus is speaking to his particular audience can be seen in that he speaks in reference to a practice and a belief held to by the Pharisees.

First, he speaks against the Pharisaical practice of divorce (Luke 16:18), a statement which at first glance seems to be out of place, but after seeing what Jesus was doing deserves as least a mention. Next, Jesus starts his final parable in a series of five with a familiar beginning, *"there was a Rich Man"* (Luke 16:19).

Once again Jesus speaks to a belief held by the Pharisees in the first century in an attempt to address the real problem. First, let's look at the teaching.

PICK YOUR VIEW

There is enough evidence to show that the Pharisees held to a peculiar view of hell—a view unsubstantiated by the Bible. While the Sadducees did not believe in the resurrection, therefore making hell a nonessential, the Pharisees believed in a resurrection and a unique teaching regarding hell. In this text Jesus is clearly zeroing in on hell, but is it intended to be a picture of hell in reality?

THE MESSAGE

Our first clue as to whether Jesus is intending to give a picture of hell's reality or speak to the false picture of hell as the Pharisees are presenting it to be is seen in the word Christ uses for hell.

The text begins, *"in hell, where he was in torment"* (Luke 16:23). Unfortunately, for those who believe this passage to be a picture of hell's reality, this text cannot be used to present an accurate view of being in torment based on the word Jesus uses in the text which is *Hades* (translated hell).[1] That Jesus uses the term *Hades* suggests that he is using someone else's word, most likely a word belonging to the Pharisees. We can be fairly certain of this based on Jesus's regular word of choice when speaking of hell in terms of judgment. Of the twelve times Jesus speaks of hell and judgment he always uses the word *Gehenna*. [2]

Hades, on the other hand, is the word that is used when speaking of the grave or place of the dead and is equal to the Old Testament word *Sheol*.[3] It makes little sense for Jesus to speak of hell as torment and use a word he's never used before for the purpose of speaking to this biblical truth.

For Christ, *Gehenna* was always spoken of as a place of judgment yet the parable of the rich man and Lazarus speaks of no judgment having occurred. They are immediately placed in an environment of torment without judgment. Nowhere in the text is there mention of the second coming (1 Cor. 15; 1 Thess. 4:13–17) or the coming of the Son of Man (Matt. 25:1–13) yet punishment has already begun. After even a cursory examination of Luke 16:19–31 one would think a type of Christian purgatory is being described more than something that is supposed to resemble *Gehenna* (hell), the final place of judgment.

LITERALLY SPEAKING

In this parable which is looking more and more like a story crafted by the Pharisees the rich man is said to be in hell (*Gehenna*), but according to their own word he is in the grave (*Hades*). The scene is described in detail. The rich man and Lazarus have both died. One is taken to a place of torment (rich man) and the other to a place far away and up (the beggar) but apparently visible to the rich man.[4]

Abraham is pictured as one attending to the needs of the beggar. Nevertheless, this picture of hell permits Abraham to talk with the rich man concerning his plight. The rich man's first request is to have the beggar come to him with a touch of relief from his suffering. He is informed that this cannot happen as they are divided by a great chasm, which prevents this communication or involvement in each other's life.

The rich man is so desperate that he longs for Lazarus to be permitted to go back to life and tell his family about this place. He argues, *"If someone comes back from the dead they will repent"* (Luke 16:30). The passage ends with Abraham telling the rich man that there's plenty of truth written in the books of Moses and the Prophets for them to believe and furthermore, *"even if someone should rise from the dead"* (Luke 16:31), they will not believe.

Clearly Jesus is speaking to the idea that the Pharisees would rather believe their own stories instead of the truth found in their own Scriptures. Having missed this it was very unlikely that they would believe in Christ even when he rises from the dead.

WHAT'S THE PROBLEM?

It's actually quite amazing that someone can take a close look at the parable of the rich man and Lazarus and reach the conclusion that this is a literal story, a painting of the most realistic picture of hell found in the Bible.

On the contrary, quite the opposite is true. Jesus uses a word to describe hell that is different from the word he has always used to speak of judgment and hell, which leads one to think that it is a borrowed story and a borrowed word. In the story Jesus describes hell as a place of interaction and dialogue, very different from the biblical picture of *Hades* (the word used here), which is the place of the dead where it is said *"the dead know nothing"* (Eccles. 9:5).

The story continues with Jesus describing hell as a place where people will be able to see others in a better place. No description is given but one is left with the impression that the beggar is in heaven or paradise. There is no mention as to how the beggar entered this place, or for that matter, how the rich man ended up in torment, except that one man (rich man) did little in his life to help the other (beggar) to better himself.

20/20 VISION

After a close examination of the parable told by Jesus in Luke 16:19–31 it would appear that Christ was not presenting a picture of hell but addressing a distorted and unbiblical teaching on hell being taught by the Pharisees. This belief is reinforced by the presence of a theological structure based on works rather than salvation or faith. There is no mention anywhere that the rich man is in hell because he didn't believe in Christ as Lord. In the end, Jesus completes his subtle but profound attack on the Pharisees by warning anyone who would teach something that would cause others to sin. Jesus says that, *"it would have been better for them to be thrown into the sea with a millstone tied around their necks than to teach false doctrine. So watch yourself"* (Luke 17:1–3).

A FINAL WORD

The words of Jesus to the Pharisees and to his disciples (Luke 17:1–3) to watch themselves is an appropriate and timely challenge even today as people continue to tire of the truth and seek to find those who will teach what they want to hear (2 Tim. 4:1–5). To accept a view of the grave or hell that violates the overall teaching on the subject would be equivalent to the mistake of the Pharisees. No one diligently wanting to handle the Word of God accurately will want to do this. So may I say, "Watch yourselves!"

12

A Grave Situation

"There is always an easy solution to every human problem: neat, plausible, and wrong!"

—H. L. Mencken

You do not have to be a biblical scholar to accurately interpret the Bible. For years, however, I have talked with people who have depended on someone else to tell them the intended meaning of a passage of Scripture without ever examining the details of the text themselves. This approach to exegesis is clear evidence of how someone can be influenced in his or her interpretation without knowing what the text actually says.

As people begin to discuss the reasons why they believe a certain way and attempt to justify their belief based upon a reasoning that bypasses the intended meaning of the text under scrutiny, it plainly reveals that their convictions come not from a balanced examination of the Bible but solely upon what somebody said they should believe.

This theological phenomenon is particularly obvious when it pertains to the Bible's teaching regarding the nature of man, Christ, and the afterlife. As expected, there are many who quote Scripture as a defense for their particular biblical view on these subjects. When it is suggested that these texts are in conflict with their belief they would rather assume the validity of these texts than go through a thorough examination of the passage in search of the truth. In the opinion of the author, the acceptance of a traditional view on these subjects by many believers has led to the defense of a biblical position that does not match the details of the supporting texts.

TO MAKE MATTERS WORSE

That there are people who want you to believe in a particular view of Scripture is not surprising in the least. The difficulty arises when it is discovered that most people believe things—even biblical teachings—simply because someone they respect or love has told them what they should believe. The pressure to believe can be intense when your grandparents and parents have held a certain view their entire lives (familial), not to mention the influence of a church (ecclesiastical), or pastor (pastoral) that have taught you to think in a certain way ever since you were young. Without realizing it, one can adopt a position on a biblical teaching and have never studied the issue at all.

DILIGENCE PAYS OFF

The apostle Paul advised young Timothy to be very careful and diligent in his handling of the word of truth (2 Tim. 2:15). He wanted Timothy to make sure that he did not give the false teachers any reason or information that could be used against the work of the Lord. On a more personal level, Timothy's understanding of the word would provide whatever Timothy needed to live a life acceptable before God (2 Tim. 3:17) and equip him to fight the false teachers but first Timothy must submit himself to the teaching, rebuking, correcting and training power of the word (2 Tim. 3:16). Only then would he be able to preach the word in a way that would meet the challenge of those who would teach unsound doctrine (2 Tim. 1:13). We too must face the evidence of the word of God especially as it pertains to those subjects we hold dear but have never studied up close and in detail.

In the following chapters we will take a careful look at many of those texts which are referenced when people seek to defend and clarify what they think the Bible teaches concerning subjects regarding the nature of man, what Christ teaches concerning death, paradise, and much, much more.

THE THIEF ON THE CROSS (Luke 23:43)

There may be another text that is quoted more often than Luke 23:43 when it comes to the idea of paradise and the question of what happens immediately after death, but I do not know what it would be. Those who support the view that a person enters the realm of *paradise* or *hell* upon death are adamant in their belief that this text supports their convictions. The text reads, *"Jesus answered him, I tell you the truth, today you will be with me in paradise"* (Luke 23:43). In order to arrive at the "truth" concerning this text we must find answers to a number of questions. Remember, it is often more important and enlightening to ask the right questions of a text rather than impose our thinking and hope that it fits.

The idea as proposed by those who suggest that the thief went directly to paradise, is that Jesus went to paradise upon his death. Is this true? Did Jesus die and go directly to paradise? If not, where did he go and how does it affect our text?

We know from the writings of the apostle John that Jesus spent a great deal of time preparing his disciples for his departure from this earth and the ministry to which he had called them. On one occasion Jesus said, *"Where I am going you cannot come"* and later *"Where I am going you cannot follow now, but you will follow later"* (John 13:33, 36). Later wasn't soon enough for Peter as we see him trying to talk Jesus into letting him go with him right then (John 13:37).

The reasons for Jesus's departure were many, but the most immediate had to do with Jesus going away to prepare a place for his disciples. He told them, *"If I go and prepare a place for you, I will come back and take you* [the disciples] *to be with me that you also may be where I am"* (John 14:2–4). The words of Jesus to his disciples in this text provide a clear picture of where Jesus was heading after his death. He was going away to prepare a place for his disciples and when he finished he would return and get his disciples so they could be with him (John 14:3).

His words here could not be any clearer. Therefore one might ask, "Why would Jesus need to return and get his disciples so they could be with him, if they are already with him?" Jesus made it clear in his priestly prayer recorded in John 17 that his intention was to return to the Father. The questions are: "When did he return to his Father? And, "Did he go immediately into the Father's presence upon his death or was it later?"

In John's gospel we read about Mary's encounter with Jesus at his grave on the third day following the crucifixion (John 20:10–17). The scene is one of grief and Mary is under the impression that Jesus's body has been stolen. She was wondering where they had taken his body when all of a sudden she was confronted by a man whom she thought was the gardener. Almost immediately Jesus spoke to her by calling her name. At this point Mary realized that the man who was talking with her was Jesus himself (John 20:16). She did what anyone in that day who loved Jesus would have done; she fell at his feet and worshipped him. She clung to him because he was her hope and he was alive!

Jesus's response to Mary's behavior provides us with specific information regarding his activity following his death on the cross. Though Mary was holding on to him, Jesus was quick to let her know that he had not returned to the Father (John 20:17). If this is true then it is appropriate to ask how Jesus could have been in paradise with the thief on the cross, beginning three days prior to this event? And how could Jesus be in paradise, and yet be here with Mary at the graveside? What are we to make of Jesus's promise to the thief on the cross about being with Him in paradise when based on these passages it would appear that Jesus did not go to paradise on that day?

First, we could conclude that Jesus lied. Perhaps he was caught up in a delusional scheme of pretending to be the Messiah and this was his last hurrah. To believe that Jesus lied would be devastating to everyone, even Jesus. To accept this option and discover that Jesus lied would mean that not only was Jesus's promise on the cross a lie, but possibly his entire life. If Jesus lied to the thief almost certainly other promises he made would become suspect.

Secondly, if Jesus did not lie, then he must have meant something else other than what is traditionally thought about his promise to the thief declaring that he would be with him in paradise on that day. No one would suggest that Jesus did not mean what he said. However, in light of biblical evidence—which reveals that Jesus had not gone back to the Father after three days in the tomb—we must conclude that Jesus was somewhere else even though he would be returning to the Father at a later date. If Jesus was not in paradise as some suggest, where was he? And, if the thief was in paradise, what kind of paradise is it if Jesus isn't there? If neither Jesus nor the thief went to paradise, where did they go?

A GRAVE SITUATION

According to the record of the gospels, Jesus was laid in a tomb or grave (Luke 23:50–53), which was provided by Joseph of Arimathea, a prominent member of the council. After receiving permission from Pilate to take the body of Jesus, Joseph, along with the women who had come with Jesus from Galilee went to the tomb and saw where Jesus's body was laid (Luke 23:55).

The practice of being laid in a grave following death was common. The Old Testament word *Sheol* is used thirty-one times to describe the place where the dead were laid. Once their life was over, each king or leader *"rested with his father"* with no mention of passing on to some other level of existence. They rested or slept with their fathers because their life was over. This is in contrast with those who consider *Sheol* to be the Old Testament word for hell but it is more likely that *Sheol* is best understood as a poetic synonym for *qeber* (grave). In the Old Testament, the grave is thought of as the resting place of all people while deliverance from *Sheol* was thought to be rescue from impending death or future punishment (Ps. 89:48).

The idea that one's hope lay solely in the grave was enough to move Job to declare, *"If the only home I hope for is the grave, if I spread out my bed in darkness, if I say to corruption, 'You are my father,' and to the worm, 'My mother' or 'My sister,' where then is my hope? Who can see any hope for me? Will it go down to the gates of death? Will we descend together into the dust?"* (Job 17:13–16). Job shared the sentiments of the Psalmist when he said, *"What man can live and not see death, or save himself from the power of the grave?"* (Ps. 89:48).

In the New Testament we find the word *Hades* being used to describe the grave. This seems clear from the text in Acts 2:27 where Peter speaks of King David's confidence that God would not abandon him to the grave (*Hades*). In this passage Peter tells us that King David, being a prophet, spoke, *"of the resurrection of the Christ, that he was not abandoned to the grave, nor did his body see decay"* (Acts 2:31). Later, the testimony of the apostle Paul confirms that Peter was not only speaking of King David's death and burial but the death, burial and resurrection of Christ. Paul states, *"For when David had served God's purpose in his own generation, he fell asleep; he was buried with his fathers and his body decayed. But the one God raised from the dead did not see decay"* (Acts 13:36–37).

The teaching that Jesus did not see decay agrees with the reports of Jesus's life after dying on the cross. Jesus did not see decay because after three days he was raised from the dead (Acts 13:34). The circumstances of Jesus's death, burial, and resurrection have definite impact for the thief on the cross. Since Jesus did not go to paradise on the day of his death, it is probable—based on the biblical evidence—that the thief like David and all others went into the grave (*Hades*) to be buried, decay, and await the resurrection of the body at the second coming.

These passages present us with a teaching that has often been overlooked when the discussion of death comes up. Mistakenly, some have taught that since Jesus died for us, death was no longer our enemy. In fact, I have often heard the words that imply that death is not an enemy but the entrance into a whole new world. The teaching that death is our friend is in complete contradiction with the words of Paul in 1 Corinthians 15:54. Here, as Paul is describing the second coming of Christ and the resurrection of our bodies he declares that death will be the last enemy destroyed. For Paul, the resurrection will bring about the end of our "decaying" process in the grave. It is at the resurrection when the "perishable" (that which decays) will be made into the "imperishable" (that which never decays) will occur (1 Cor. 15:54). Only then will death see its own ruin. Only then will death have no more power over mankind, seen clearly in Paul's statement, "*Then the saying that is written will come true: Death has been swallowed up in victory. Where, O death, is your victory? Where, O death, is your sting?*" (1 Cor. 15:54–55). According to the apostle John's vision on the Isle of Patmos, death and Hades will meet their final demise at the judgment seat of God when, "*death and Hades were thrown into the lake of fire. The lake of fire is the second death*" (Rev. 20:13–14). Only then will death have no more power.

SEE YOU LATER

After a thorough study of Christ's experience with the thief on the cross (Luke 23:43), we have been able to determine at least three truths regarding the words spoken there.

First, we recognize that Jesus was speaking these words in order to encourage the thief based upon his belief in Christ. Jesus wanted the thief to know that even though he had spent his entire life living for the enemy he could now find hope in Christ. His life was soon to be over yet Christ promised him on that day that when he established his kingdom the thief would be a part of that great crowd of witnesses to God's grace.

Secondly, the promise Jesus gave the thief was not realized on that day based on our discovery that Jesus did not go to paradise on the day of his death. Instead, Jesus entered the place of the dead, the grave (*Sheol* or *Hades*). For three days Jesus lay in the grave with no activity or thought. He did not according to his own words go back to the Father during this time. Instead, he slept and awaited his own resurrection. This means that Jesus did not go to paradise and neither did the thief. He too went into the grave and is awaiting the resurrection of the body (1 Cor. 15:22). At that time those who have been in the grave will be made alive but not until then.

Finally, the promise Jesus gave the thief is a promise for you and me today. Our death will not mean an immediate transportation into the presence of God in paradise. Jesus must first return and get us so that where he is we may be also (John 14:3). This means that the words spoken by Jesus on the cross to the thief would be best rendered in this way: "*I tell you the truth today, you will be with me in paradise*" (Luke 23:43). These words gave the thief hope as he hung on his cross. May these be words of encouragement and hope for you today as you carry your cross (Luke 14:27).

13

To Die or Not to Die?

"I intend to live forever, or die trying!"

—Anonymous

As a young boy, I was a little shy of going to a funeral home. I suspect that it had something to do with the fact that I attended my very first funeral in a funeral home. Those places can be kind of scary for a young boy. Besides, having to come to grips with death was not high on my list of things to do.

The fact that someone died was not a "big deal" for me as a kid. No one really close to me had ever died. However, as the years went by I had reason to take a closer look at this life event especially on the occasion of my grandfather's death. It didn't take long to realize that Granddaddy was not coming back. But where did he go? What happened to him? Would I see him again? These were questions that flooded my mind and I eagerly looked for the answers.

Being raised in the church provided some direction for me regarding these questions. Unfortunately, what I discovered was a series of "pat" answers to some difficult inquiries. I longed for some kind of clear evidence that would point me in the right direction regarding these matters. I soon discovered that the answers that seem so simple to people in my church didn't match the information I was receiving from others.

Soon I realized that not everyone thought the same way about what happens to people when they die. I had always been told that when people die they are laid in a grave and await the second coming of Christ, yet others were telling me that when you die a spiritual part of you (the *real you* in their words) goes to "heaven" to be with God. I wondered if that's what happened to my grandfather? Was Granddaddy in heaven? Is that what will happen to me? I wanted to know.

The reality of death eventually hits everyone. I can't imagine that there is someone living today who hasn't been touched by this life event. However, having someone close to you die is nothing like dealing with your own death. In recent years there have been people who have been pronounced clinically dead but returned to the land of the living only to proclaim that they have been to "heaven." Quite honestly, there's not much I can say about this kind of experience since I wasn't there. There's no way I can refute or affirm the testimony of such a person. They could say anything and I would never be able to prove that it didn't happen. The fact that someone says, "This is what happened to me," does not make it true or an accurate portrayal of what happens to people when they die. The only direction I have is the word of God. The true litmus test for the reliability of such a testimony is whether or not it agrees with the teaching of the Bible.

TO DIE OR NOT TO DIE

The idea that you don't actually die when you die is somewhat confusing to me. The Old Testament teaches that when a person's life was over, it was over. On many occasions the writers of the Bible, especially Job, David and Solomon declared that the dead know nothing (Job 14:7–12, 17:13–16; Ps. 6:4–5, 30:9, 49:12, 14, 88:11–12, 115:17, 146: 1–4; Eccles. 9:5–6, 10). If the dead know nothing then how could anyone who has died and lived again say anything about what happened to them during their death? Could it be that what Solomon declared as upright and true (Eccles. 12:10) was false? Could it be that God would give Solomon the gift of wisdom and inspire him to write something that was untrue?

Those who believe this kind of spiritual "oxymoron" (dead but not dead) often refer to the apostle Paul's words in the book of Philippians which reads, *"For to me, to live is Christ and to die is gain. If I am to go on living in the body, this will mean fruitful labor for me. Yet what shall I choose? I do not know! I am torn between the two: I desire to depart and be with Christ, which is better by far; but it is more necessary for you that I remain in the body"* (Phil. 1:21–23). While at first glance this Scripture seems to suggest that Paul was advocating a view that when this physical life is over the "real" person is released from the body and immediately enters into the presence of God, it deserves a closer look.

TO FLY OR NOT TO FLY

Have you ever noticed that some of the best songs are built on "bad" theology? I can still remember a former professor in Bible College saying that he chose not to sing a song like "He Lives" for this very reason. The chorus goes like this: *"You ask me how I know he lives. He lives within my heart."* While it is true that Jesus lives within our hearts (John 14:21–23; Rom. 10:9–10), it is not the reason we know he lives. We know that he lives because the Bible tells us so. The belief that he lives within our heart is a confirmation of this biblical fact. The end result was that the professor would not sing something he did not think and believe was true.

While some refuse to sing songs that aren't true, others sing songs that they do not understand. One such song is "Come Thou Fount of Every Blessing" (lyrics by Robert Robinson, 1735–1790). In this song Robinson writes these words in the beginning of the second verse, *"Here I raise my Ebenezer; Hither by thy help I'm come; And I hope, by thy good pleasure, Safely to arrive at home."*[1] I find it interesting that most people have no idea what an Ebenezer is yet they have sung this song for years. That this is a confusing word is hinted at by the rewriting of these words in the 1997 version of *The Celebration Hymnal* by Margaret Clarkson. In this version, verse two begins: *"Hither to thy love hast blest me; Thou has bro't me to this place; And I know thy hand will bring me safely home by thy good grace."*[2]

It seems obvious that the reason Margaret Clarkson changed the words was due to the fact that many people had no clue as to what an Ebenezer was. The truth is that an Ebenezer is a memorial stone placed in the location where God has been our help, a marker of God's faithfulness (1 Sam. 7:1–12). Certainly this is true for every believer and is worthy of being sung about but it is also important to know what you're singing.

Another song that conjures up this kind of response for some is "I'll Fly Away." This song has an upbeat tempo and many proclaim, "What's the harm in singing it even if you don't believe what it says?" I confess to you that perhaps there's no harm, but more importantly I would propose another question: "Is it true?" Do we fly away when this life is over? Is this what Paul is teaching in Philippians or is there something here that we are missing? Are we singing something that we know is true or simply singing a song that sounds good?

PRISON THOUGHTS

I can remember clearly the early days of my first pastorate. Like any pastor, I wanted to do the very best I could do in proclaiming the teaching of the Bible. On one occasion I made the decision to preach on the passage of Scripture written by Paul in 2 Timothy 2:8–10 where Paul speaks of being chained like a criminal.

The only way I could think of getting into the real sense of this text was to experience the "being chained like a criminal" part. Maybe then I would understand what Paul was saying. Fortunately, I lived in New England where most of the houses have basements. The one we lived in not only had a basement, it had a creepy, dirty, and somewhat scary basement. It had beams that served as support for the house and a whole lot of clutter that had been stored down there for years. In all honestly it was more like a dungeon than a basement. Nevertheless I thought it would serve as a perfect site for a prison experience.

You can imagine the reaction of my young bride when I told her my idea: "*You're going to do what?*" So off I went into the dark confines of my "prison." I even had my wife chain me to a pole and bring me bread and water every couple of hours. I can't remember how long I stayed down there, but it was most of a day. What I do remember is how I felt and some of the things that went through my mind. Being on your back in the dirt, darkness, and a place crawling with bugs has a way of making you think about a lot of things.

You may laugh at my experiment but it was quite revealing to me. I discovered some important things about myself and about the apostle Paul. I can understand why Paul might reach the point where he was more concerned about the gospel and its integrity than his well-being. It would be very easy to resign yourself at some point to never getting out of prison. Paul had accepted the possibility that this might be the end of his life and he was willing to accept that reality.

Some suggest that Paul's language in this text supports the idea that he believed in an immediate departure from life in the body and into the presence of Christ (Phil. 1:23). No one would argue that Paul was not in a difficult position in prison and perhaps even thinking that this would be the end of his life and ministry. It is not surprising to hear him talk about being torn between two possibilities: remaining in the body or departing and being with Christ (Phil. 1:23). If these verses were taken at face value then it would appear that Paul believed in an immediate departure into the presence of God at the time of his death. But is this the total picture?

RESURRECTION ON MY MIND

Departing and being with Christ was not the only thing on Paul's mind as Philippians 3:10 will confirm. Here, Paul testifies that he would sacrifice everything just to know Christ and to be a recipient of his righteousness through faith (Phil. 3:9). He wanted *"to know Christ and the power of his resurrection and the fellowship of sharing in his sufferings, becoming like him in his death, and so, somehow, to attain to the resurrection from the dead"* (Phil. 3:9–11).

In the very next verse Paul declares that this is *not* something he has already obtained (Phil. 3:12). He hoped for it. Nevertheless Paul knew that he was by faith a member of that community of Christ's followers that one day would welcome a Savior, returning from the Father (John 14:1–4) and at that time his body would be transformed into a glorious body like the body of his Lord (Phil. 3:21).

LET ME LOOSE!

If a person takes every word of the Bible at face value without determining if it fits into the context or not it can be very misleading. In view of our text (Phil. 1:18–25), does Paul really believe that he will join Christ immediately upon his death? Are we to understand that simply because Paul uses the word "depart" in connection to being with Christ that it is an instantaneous event? A further examination of this text might prove otherwise.

BREAKING LOOSE

The word depart in the Greek language (Grk. *analuo*/*analusai*) is an interesting word and worth our exploration. This form of the word depart is only found in Philippians 1:23 and carries with it the idea of being "loosed or untied." This interpretation of the word comes from its root meaning in a metaphor drawn from the work of loosing from moorings preparatory to setting sail. Young's Analytical Concordance mentions the idea of loosing up an anchor (pg. 245).

Luke uses a form of this word in the book of Acts (16:26) when he describes the breaking "loose" of the chains following the violent midnight earthquake that set Paul and Silas free from jail in Philippi. Here one can see the sense in which the word "depart" simply means to be let go. Paul and Silas were released from their chains and put into a position where they could leave the jail.

In Paul's letter to the Christians at Philippi it is not difficult to see that his number one concern was the preaching of Christ through the gospel (Phil. 1:18). He wanted nothing to interfere with this desire. Even though Paul thought that he would be delivered from prison (Phil. 1:19), the possibility of his death was not out of the question. Therefore, his goal became that even in his death Christ would be exalted (Phil. 1:21).

It is not difficult to see from Paul's words in Colossians 3:4 that every believer finds their "life" through Christ or as rendered in Philippians 1:21: *"For to me, to live is Christ.*" Paul knew that the most productive way for him to continue to bring glory and honor to God was through his faithful living and his continued labors with Christians like the ones in Philippi. He also knew that even should he die, that too, could bring glory and honor to Christ.

The word Paul uses in Philippians 1:21 to speak of his death and its potential advancement of the gospel is a Greek word which refers to dying. The actual word, *apothanein*, is an aorist infinitive of *thnesko*. That Paul uses an aorist infinitive argues that he is not talking about the act of dying but rather that he has died. The proper way to translate this word then becomes "to have died" (see Kenneth Wuest, Philippians in the New Testament, pg. 45). Paul was simply saying that even when he dies Christ will be exalted.

The idea that the apostle Paul might want to leave or be loosed (pull up his anchor) from his work with the Philippian believers is not hard to understand. His service to the Lord was quite different than that for a modern day believer. When's the last time you were in prison for the fact that you loved Jesus? When were you last in danger of losing your life because you preached the gospel message? Clearly one cannot suggest that Paul was just tired and getting old therefore he wanted to die and be done with it altogether. On the contrary, Paul was trying to make it clear to the believers that whatever happened he wanted Christ to be exalted and the gospel to be treated in a worthy manner (Phil. 1:27).

IT ALL FITS

The strongest argument for understanding Paul's words in Philippians 1:18–25 in this way is that this understanding fits within the broader context of Paul's writings in the New Testament. The only other place in the New Testament where Paul uses language similar to Philippians 1 is in 2 Corinthians 5:8–10. Here the apostle Paul speaks of "*being away from the body and at home with the Lord*" and "*so we make it our goal to please him, whether we are at home in the body or away from it.*" These words are given context with the words that follow them arguing strongly that we will all appear before the Lord at the judgment seat of Christ. First Corinthians 15 and Matthew 25:31 provide a more specific picture of when this judgment seat will take place. People will not appear before the judgment seat of God until Christ returns. At that time and no sooner will our bodies be changed into bodies fit for the kingdom of God.

The thought given by many that death is a friend or a passageway into an immediate presence with the Lord does not stand up under the close scrutiny of the Scriptures. For example, further along in Paul's writings to the Philippian believers he speaks of his friendship with Epaphroditus, a brother and co-worker in the Lord (Phil. 3:25) who had been very sick, even unto death.

If death is to be seen as a doorway into paradise or heaven isn't it interesting that Paul states that Epaphroditus was shown "mercy" by the Lord in preventing his death through his healing (Phil. 3:27). In addition, Paul states that he too was spared from sorrow upon sorrow (Phil. 3:27) by Epaphroditus' healing. From this text alone one can see that death is not to be seen as the blissful exit from life into an immediate life in heaven but simply the end of one's labors until Christ shall come.

A GREAT CLOUD OF WITNESSES

Paul's death, should it occur, would place him with others who were also awaiting the coming of the Lord. According to the writer of Hebrews this included a great throng of people, even giants in the faith, who were willing to endure shame, pain and even death, "*so that they might gain a better resurrection*" (Heb. 11:35). This resurrection will not come until Christ returns (1 Cor. 15). The author of Hebrews declares that while each of these men and women were commended for their faith and the way they lived their lives, "*none of them received what they had been promised. God had planned something better for us so that only together with us would they be made perfect*" (Heb. 11:39–40).

The idea of being made perfect appears to be very similar to Paul's yearning for his body to be transformed into a body like the body of Jesus and sounds very much like the words of the apostle Paul written to Timothy in what most people believe to be his parting words. He realized that the end was near and it was almost time for his departure. He had fought a good fight, finished the race, and kept the faith (2 Tim. 4: 6–7). It is tempting to think that Paul is talking about departing in the sense of leaving this life when he dies but the words that follow clarify his message.

In Paul's own words he declares that he would join that great cloud of witnesses spoken of in Hebrews. At the end of his life Paul, along with everyone who has put his or her faith in Christ, will receive a "*crown of righteousness, which the Lord will award to him [me] on that day—and not only to me, but also to all who have longed for his appearing*" (2 Tim. 4:8–9). Paul was not putting himself before anyone else who called Jesus Lord. He knew the order, "*For as in Adam all die, all will be made alive But each in his own turn: Christ, the firstfruits, then, when he comes, those who belong to him*" (1 Corinthians 15:22–23).

TENTS, CLOTHES, AND JARS OF CLAY

Serving God was a way of life for Paul. Ever since Christ met him on the road to Damascus Paul had committed his life to the preaching of the gospel. It was this message that gave Paul's life meaning and made it possible for him to endure anything, even death.

Paul realized that not everyone shared his belief in Christ. Nevertheless he was determined to preach the gospel in an effort to bring people into a saving relationship with the Lord. This was the difference according to Paul. He wanted to know Christ. The knowledge of Christ in the heart and mind of the believer was the determining factor for those who believed. The ones who chose not to believe, in Paul's mind, were being deceived by *"the god of this age"* (2 Cor. 4:4) and prevented from seeing the *"the light of the gospel of the glory of Christ, who is the image of God"* (2 Cor. 4:4b).

For Paul the treasure inside each believer is *"the knowledge of the glory of God in the face of Christ"* (2 Cor. 4:6). It is knowing that Christ will never leave you or forsake you (Heb. 13:5); it is knowing that no matter what light and momentary troubles are happening to you, they are achieving an eternal glory that far outweighs them all (2 Cor. 4:17). It is knowing that even though your journey in life will end in death (2 Cor. 5:1) that one day this mortal life will be clothed in immortality (1 Cor. 15:54–55) and we will be at home with the Lord (2 Cor. 5:9). It is not surprising at all that Paul yearned for this day.

DON'T BE IGNORANT

While it's tempting to believe what others say it is more important to read the Bible and discover the truth for yourself. It is essential that all believers develop a biblical viewpoint regarding those issues that matter the most. Apparently, in the first century the believers were beginning to worry about the status of those who had fallen asleep (1 Thess. 4:13). Not wanting them to be ignorant of these things Paul attempted to remove their confusion. His message to the believers included at least three truths:

First, the death, burial and resurrection of Christ insure that one day he will reunite us with those who have died (1 Thess. 4:14). It is because of his victory over death and the grave that we have hope for our own future. He is the first-fruits of the resurrection guaranteeing our resurrection at the second coming.

Second, those who are alive when Jesus returns will not precede those who have fallen asleep in death. This means that the dead have not already gone to be with the Lord, if they have not risen yet. Their resurrection will take place when the archangel shouts and the trumpet call of God takes place. According to Paul's words to the Corinthians, this will take place at the second coming (1 Cor. 15:52).

Third, after the dead in Christ rise then those who are still alive will join everyone in the clouds to meet the Lord and at that point we will be with the Lord forever (1 Thess. 4:17–18).

I can understand why the early believers would be confused and concerned about their loved ones. I began this chapter in the same way. I wondered about the status of my grandfather. Years later now, I have the same interest in my dad and my sister. Where are they? Will I see them again? Absolutely!

They are resting from their labors in the grave. One day however Christ will return and they will rise to be with him forever more. One day, should we still be alive, we too will hear his voice calling us to be with Him. While it is tempting to believe that this hope is realized at the point of our death the Scriptures say otherwise. So until then, *"we wait for the blessed hope-the glorious appearing of our great God and Savior, Jesus Christ"* (Titus 2:13).

14

For Better or Worse

"We make a living by what we get out of life, but we make a life by what we give!"

—Anonymous

Of all the chapters in the Bible, I consider the eleventh chapter of Hebrews my favorite. There are many reasons for this but the overwhelming factor in my choice is that the writer of Hebrews presents the life of faith through real people. The stars of this chapter include a mixture of patriarchs, prophets, and even prostitutes who trusted God by living lives of faith. Not one of these men and women had the advantage when it came to living their lives before God. Each one was required to demonstrate their commitment to God through faith.

Faith is the common denominator in those who desire to serve God for without faith it is impossible to please God (Heb. 11:6). Even so, while each person in Hebrews 11 was described as a person of faith a point was reached in their lives when they had to make a decision to live out their faith or choose the easier path of less resistance. Time and time again, we read about the challenges they faced. They were tested, tortured, tormented, and even torn apart. Yet, they endured and trusted God completely.

DEAD, BUT NOT FORGOTTEN

The writer of Hebrews interjects within the text on more than one occasion that these men and women never fully received, *"the things promised; they only saw them from a distance"* (Heb. 11:13). All of these faithful warriors fought to the very end of their lives for what they believed and were still seeking for these things by faith even when they died.

In dying they proved that they were *"longing for a better country-a heavenly one"* (Heb. 11:16). Hoping for *"a better resurrection"* (Heb. 11:36), they served until the end and were commended for their faith (Heb. 11:39). Interestingly though and contrary to popular belief they did not receive what they were promised after they died either. The writer makes it perfectly clear that God had *"planned something better for us so that only together with us would they be made perfect"* (Heb. 11:40).

This is an amazing thought to consider. Take a look at this list of men and women and you will find that it is easy to be overwhelmed with the idea that one day we will come before our God and receive our reward for faith with them. Not only are we looking forward to the day when we will join these saints before the Lord but until then we are encouraged by the writer of Hebrews to remember these examples of faith in order that we too might be found faithful in the living of our lives.

A LESSON LEARNED

Because God was planning a time for those who lived by faith to be made perfect suggests that prior to that time they were not perfect. This agrees with Paul's revelation that *"all have sinned and fallen short of God's glory"* (Rom. 3:23). Until that time man is bound by the limitations of his mortality and subject to the consequences held for those who do not know Christ as Lord. No one who fails to meet God's expectations will be permitted to remain in his presence eternally, *"for our God is a consuming fire"* (Heb. 12:29).

Here the writer to the Hebrews draws upon an experience in the life of Israel when they were prone to give themselves over to the worship of man-made idols. Moses warns the people of God that they should be very careful not to pursue this life, for their God *"is a consuming fire, a jealous God"* (Deut. 4:24). Even if they made it into the Promised Land, the people of Israel were told be faithful to this command or else suffer the consequence of destruction (Deut. 4:26). If they disobeyed, they would surely *"perish from the land"* (Deut. 4:26).

BY FAITH ALONE

If living by faith is the only way to please God then all other efforts fall short. While *"faith without deeds is dead"* (James 2:18, 26), deeds without faith is dead too. Who then can stand in his presence? And, even more importantly, if one falls short of God's glory and never comes to God in faith, what then? What does the future hold for such a person? Can they continue to live? How can one who fails to please God remain in his presence eternally? Won't he or she be consumed in the presence of a God who is a consuming fire? Can a person that is bound by the limits of his own sinful mortality live forever in the presence of a Holy God and not perish? The truth is that Christ came into the world to make it possible that no one would perish (John 3:16). The sad reality is that those without Christ will. Paul wrote of this in his letter to the Christians in Rome by declaring that the *"wages of sin is death, but the gift of God is eternal life in Christ Jesus our Lord"* (Rom. 6:23). While those who profess faith in Christ will receive the gift of a fully realized eternal life or immortality when He comes, those who deny him will perish and live no more.

HOW HOT IS HELL?

The most familiar and perhaps greatest verse in the entire Bible tells us that God gave his Son in order to prevent man from perishing (John 3:16). In this verse John presents our options: believe in Christ and live forever or deny him and per- ish. This verse alone makes it clear that God is the giver of life and the one who can take it away. John affirms these words found in his gospel account when he proclaims that the only person who has life in any form is the person who gives his life to Christ in faith (1 John 5:12). Only in Christ does man have life. With- out Christ man will not have life. He will perish and no longer exist. He will not be tormented forever but be gone.

If then, hell is meant for destruction (2 Thess. 1:9) one would be surprised to find out that hell is not hot enough to destroy whatever is placed in it. Jesus made a clear distinction between hell as the grave (Hades) and hell as the place of judg- ment and destruction (*Gehenna*). In Matthew 10:28 Jesus warns his disciples against the real enemy known as the second death (Rev. 20:14–15) that will take place in Gehenna hell. In light of this truth they should not fear someone who can kill the body and not the soul. Rather, they should fear the one who can kill both the body and the soul.

Jesus is talking about the whole person dying in the fires of hell never to live again. The prophet Ezekiel testifies that the *"soul who sins is the one who will die"* in contrast with the man who *"is righteous; he will surely live, declares the Sovereign Lord"* (Ezek. 18:4, 20). Since his name is written in the book of life the believer in Christ will not be thrown into the lake of fire (Rev. 20:15). His future is secure due to the saving work of Christ on the cross and through his victory over death for God so loved the world that he gave his only Son as a ransom (a correspond- ing price) for all who would believe (John 3:16; 1 Tim. 2:4–6) so that they would not perish (forever cease to live). As man was appointed to die as a result of his sin

(Heb. 9:27) so also Christ was destined to die for man in order to free him from the bondage of his sin and prevent his everlasting destruction.

WHEN AND WHERE?

Since man is mortal and cannot continue to live without God's permission or provision he is destined to live or perish depending on his relationship with Jesus Christ. If man chooses *not* to confess with his mouth, *"Jesus is Lord,"* and *not* believe in his heart that *"God raised him from the dead,"* (Rom. 10:9–10) he will *not* be saved and he will *not* live forever.

According to the Scriptures judgment will take place sometime after death and at the time of Christ's appearing a second time (Matt. 25). The Psalmist speaks of judgment day as the time when the faithfulness of the godly will be rewarded and the *"way of the wicked will perish"* (Ps. 1:1–6). On *"that day"* (2 Tim. 1:18) those who love God will be blessed and recognized for their commitment to God as well as their love and service for God (Matt. 25:34–40) while those who rejected Christ and his ways will be singled out and sent into the fires of hell to experience eternal punishment (Matt. 25:46).

We know from the writings of Jude that the idea of an eternal fire does not necessarily include the thought that the fire goes on forever and ever but rather that the result of the fire's destruction is eternal. In Jude 7, Sodom and Gomorrah are given as examples of those who chose to live a life of perversion and ungodliness rather than trust in God. Jude writes that these cities and their destruction serve as an example of what happens to those who *"suffer the punishment of eternal fire"* (Jude 7).

It is clear from the text and our understanding of history that Sodom and Gomorrah no longer exist. These cities and the people who dwelt in them suffered the consequence of rejecting God. You cannot travel to the location of these two cities today and watch their continued burning. They have been destroyed. Jude wanted his readers to understand clearly that those who rejected God in Sodom and Gomorrah no longer exist nor does the fire that destroyed them. His point is clear and serves as an example for you and for me. If we choose to reject the grace of God in this life we too will suffer the punishment of an eternal fire, not one that goes on forever and ever but one that brings an eternal result.

HELL'S FURY

The Bible does not picture hell as a place where nothing happens. As in the garbage dump around Jerusalem where the daily trash was placed to be burned, and destroyed, so also will those whose "*name was not found written in the book of life*" be thrown into the lake of fire, which is the second death (Rev. 20:14–15). Death and Hades will also be thrown into the lake of fire to be punished by extinction. One cannot think that death and Hades will experience eternal pain in the lake. Instead, these two enemies of God's people will be gone forever. Death will be swallowed up in victory (1 Cor. 15:54–56) and death will reign no more (Rev. 21:4).

Just as God's curse will be poured out on those who reject him, his blessings will be showered on those who by faith have entered into his kingdom (Matt. 25:34; John 3:5–6). In the end God will make all things new by creating a new heaven and new earth fit for his people, where "*he will live with them. They will be his people and God himself will be with them and be their God*" (Rev. 21:3–4). Indeed, God will make all things new (Rev. 21:5). You can count on it (Rev. 21:5b).

15

For Heaven's Sake!

"The grand essentials to happiness in this life are something to do, someone to love, and something to hope for!"

—Joseph Addison

I've never been to heaven and I've never met someone who's been there either. So it's quite difficult talking about something that I know little about. And yet throughout my life I have heard preachers preach and people talk about the "fact" that people go to heaven when they die. For years, I have listened to and even sung the lyrics of songs that proclaim the belief in an immediate hereafter, in a land beyond the sky. But is this true?

Since man is pictured as a mere mortal in the Scriptures, is it reasonable to expect that he will live beyond the grave without having been given the ability to exist eternally? How can man, who does not have the intrinsic power to continue living beyond the grave, move into a realm of existence he is not fit for (1 Cor. 15:40)?

Ever since the early church was founded, the matter of man's immediate destiny following death has been in question. Unfortunately, the Bible is virtually silent when it comes to presenting a clearly defined theology of heaven, leaving one to make the most of those biblical passages that speak in any way to the matter of life beyond the grave. The literature of the first and second centuries, especially that of the early church fathers, provide evidence that most people believed that this life was all there was until the resurrection which would take place in the future (John 11:24).[1]

The belief that heaven is not a literal place where believers go immediately upon death is a logical carry-over of the teaching found in the Old Testament regarding this subject, which is essentially nonexistent. Nowhere in the Old Testament do we find the modern day teaching that man flies off to be with the Lord at death. Instead, over and over again, the writers of the Old Testament declare their confidence in a God who would not forsake them but return one day to redeem his people. Job, led by the Holy Spirit, declared his certainty concerning the return of his Redeemer believing that he would see him in his "flesh." That Job speaks of seeing God in his flesh suggests the idea of a time when Job will be able to "see" God (Job 19:25–27).

According to John the apostle, this will take place not at the point of death but when Christ appears for only then will we "*be like him, for we shall see him as he is*" (1 John 3:2). This same thought is seen in the well-known words of the apostle Paul regarding the second coming of Christ when he proclaims that "*flesh and blood cannot inherit the Kingdom of God, nor does the perishable inherit the imperishable*" (1 Cor. 15:50). The average believer probably expects to go to heaven at death but the reality is that this truth is not proposed or taught in the Bible's use of the word heaven.

MODERN DAY CONJECTURE

The near silence on the subject of heaven in the Bible has led to the creation of a variety of views regarding its true nature. Given the level of biblical literacy among believers in general and specifically regarding a specific topic, most (believers) cannot articulate clearly what the Bible has to say about this subject. As a result it is no wonder that a multitude of thoughts concerning heaven exist today even among the church.

It is at this point that one realizes just how influential the culture can be in the development of what a person thinks and believes. In years past, much of the theology of the day came from the pulpit. In no way did this guarantee that the proclamation was true but the likelihood of it being Bible-centered was increased significantly. In recent years as surveys reveal, many pastors do not possess what is called a "biblical worldview"[2] and in itself argues for a way of thinking that comes not from being rooted in God's Word but rather from a source that is anthropocentric or in other words, worldly.

BEWARE OF EMOTIONS

While it is true that God created us as emotional creatures, it is extremely dangerous to allow our emotions to be the determining factor in the development of a biblical theology on any subject. Theology that is accepted because it is what we want to "think" happens may be comforting to us but entirely miss the teaching of the Bible.

I am reminded of a time when a man said to me in response to hearing the idea that the dead do not go to heaven immediately upon their death, *"I don't care what the Bible says, I get great comfort thinking that my mom is with Jesus."* I responded by stating that this thought might bring him comfort but the fact that you think this way does not mean that your view represents the teaching of the Scriptures.

SING ME A SONG

Throughout history people have written and sung songs in an attempt to communicate what they feel and think about every aspect of life. It is not surprising then to find people expressing themselves in song regarding the issues of life such as death and more particularly what happens after death. These are some of the most emotional and traumatic times in a person's life. Unsurprisingly, in times like these we want to think the very best thoughts for the one who has died. How else would we be able to comfort? Sometimes, if we spoke about what we really think represents reality the entire situation would change.

The idea that we are prone to project our hopes and thoughts into our theology is seen in my recent discovery of two gospel songs. Each song in its own way demonstrates an effort to convey comfort by pulling on the emotional heartstrings of the people who listen while at the same time bypassing the teaching of the Bible.

The first song is entitled "Jesus has a Rocking Chair." Nothing can be more emotionally packed than when a parent loses a child. It seems quite clear from the Scriptures and the way of life that parents are to die first, then the kids. When the order is reversed, we feel the pain. We long to hold that precious child whether they are young or grown and tell them that we love them. If it were possible we would gladly take their pain.

The problem with songs like "Jesus Has a Rocking Chair" is that it is a beautiful song. It stirs the heart of anyone whether they have lost a child or not. The story line of the song suggests that we don't have to worry about the child because Jesus has a rocking chair in heaven. He will take care of the child supposedly until the real mom arrives at her point of death. Is it really true that Jesus has a rocking chair? Is Jesus literally rocking every child that is said to be in heaven? Is he rocking them one by one or does he have a rocking chair big enough to rock them all at once? I understand clearly that the song is somewhat like a metaphor representing the idea that God will take care of those we cannot. But again I must ask, "Is this really true?"

The second song takes the idea of projecting our thoughts and longings to another level. This song is entitled, "If There's a Phone in Heaven, Please Put Momma on the Line." I must admit that the first time I heard this song I chuckled. Can you imagine the scene? Over the loudspeaker in heaven we might hear, "There's a long-distance call on line one for Momma Warren. It's your son!"

The only reason someone might write such a song is that they already think Momma is in heaven. They obviously miss Momma and long to tell her that they love her. Are there phones in heaven? I don't think so! However, once again we see in this song the projection of one's deepest thoughts, which in many people's eyes equal truth.

The thinking behind this cultural phenomenon is circular. It goes something like this. This is a wonderful singing group and they love the Lord very much. I have loved their songs for years so why would I think that they are going to sing something that is not true. Why would I not agree with the message of their songs? I trust them to sing about truth. Besides, it is a beautiful song. It must be true; therefore I will accept it without knowing whether or not it is biblical.

Slowly and surely we find ourselves accepting songs and even preaching and teaching that in no way represents the picture portrayed in the pages of Scripture. It is quite easy to suggest a particular teaching from a given text if no other text is studied. Time and time again the basic principle of "let Scripture interpret Scripture" is violated when seeking the truth. Even in our exegesis we are often guilty of reading into a text our preferred interpretation rather than allowing the text to speak for itself. One subject that has been distorted by this approach is the biblical teaching on heaven. For this reason alone it deserves a closer look.

FOR HEAVEN'S SAKE!

All my life I have heard people say, "Well, for heaven's sake!" when responding to good or bad news. For the most part I see this as a simple way of reacting to something that surprises or shocks a person. The mere statement itself suggest that one thinks of another place called heaven that is worthy of consideration as we seek to live our lives.

This line of thinking fits well with the words of the apostle Paul in Colossians 3:1–4. Here Paul exhorts the believers to "*set their hearts on things above, where Christ is seated at the right hand of God. Set your minds on things above, not on earthly things.*" Indeed, Paul would agree that we should live "for heaven's sake!" Paul understood that since coming to Christ in faith, "*our citizenship is in heaven*" (Phil. 3:20), yet he also accepted that we must live this way until Christ returns at which time we will appear with Him in glory (Col. 3:4), but not until then. Until then, we eagerly await his arrival (Phil. 3:20).

The Bible presents the challenge of living faithfully for God in very clear terms. Even upon Christ's departure from this world the angel of God made it clear that we are to live faithful lives until he returns. We are to be his witnesses throughout the world. The angel declared, "*This same Jesus, who has been taken from you into heaven, will come back in the same way you have seen him go into heaven*" (Acts 1:11), suggesting that the disciples should be busy with God's work until He returns.

Jesus spoke similar words to his disciples in John 14:1–4. Here Jesus spoke words of promise in an attempt to encourage his disciples at the sight of their discouragement. They were told not to be disheartened, for even though Jesus was leaving he would be back to get them. This was the very reason for his leaving. He was going away in order to get things ready for them. He was going away but he would be back in order to get them so they could be with him (Acts 1:11; 1 Thess. 1:10; 2 Thess. 1:7). It seems quite clear that if Jesus was coming back to get them so they could be with Him that prior to His coming back they were not with Him.

THE KINGDOM OF HEAVEN

Heaven, according to the New Testament is a timeless and location-less concept identified as the "kingdom of heaven." Of the thirty-one times this phrase is used by New Testament writers, not one refers to a place where people go when they die either to await the resurrection or after the resurrection has taken place. Instead, heaven is pictured as the realm of God into which the believer enters and exists by placing his or her trust in Christ (John 3:3–5) and is prepared for by storing up "*treasurers in heaven*" that cannot be destroyed (Matt. 6:20) and by knowing that whatever is done or experienced here on earth, be it humility (Matt. 5:3) or persecution (Matt. 5:10), will be rewarded in the realm of God known as the kingdom of heaven.

UP CLOSE AND PERSONAL

By seeing Christ, one was able to see the Father and in so doing know something about his kingdom. On one occasion Jesus told his listeners that the "kingdom of heaven" was near. What they didn't know was that the ambassador of this kingdom was in their midst and the kingdom he referred to was very near (Matt. 3:2).

Throughout his life Jesus brought the nature of God's kingdom into view for all to see. Once, when Phillip was wondering about when he would get to see the Father of this kingdom, Jesus responded by telling him, *"Anyone who has seen me has seen the Father"* (John 14:9).

The idea that the Bible talks a lot about heaven as a place where the dead go is simply not true. God's Kingdom reign on earth through Christ and his continued reign through the church will one day be established for eternity but not until Christ returns to claim them.

In the New Testament heaven is seen as that supernatural sphere in which God dwells and from which he governs both heaven and earth (Matt. 11:25). Periodically in the life of Jesus we see the kingdom of heaven entering into the kingdom of this world by way of miracles which were viewed by those whom Jesus taught as *"a sign from heaven"* (Matt. 16:1).

A NEW HEAVEN AND A NEW EARTH

Jesus entered this world in order to give us hope for a new world, one that operated by his principles. This desire can be seen in the way Jesus taught his disciples to pray saying, *"your kingdom come, your will be done on earth as it is in heaven"* (Matt. 6:10). But when will this prayer be answered? When will God's kingdom be fully established for God's people to enjoy it? Do God's people enter into this type of kingdom at the point of death? Has Jesus already set up his kingdom before he returns to earth the second time? If not now, when? Exactly when will God's people enjoy his kingdom?

According to both the Old and New Testaments, God will at some point in time create a new heaven and a new earth (Isa. 65:17). The exact timing of this transformation is revealed in 2 Peter 3:7, 10–13 as being at the end of the age when *"The heavens will disappear with a roar; the elements will be destroyed by fire, and the earth and everything in it will be laid bare"* (2 Pet. 3:10). Just as the earth was destroyed by water through the flood, the heavens and the earth are being held for another form of destruction; fire (2 Pet. 3:7).

John the apostle unfolds this eschatological event in Revelation 21:1–4. Here he describes *"a new heaven and a new earth, for the first heaven had passed away, and there was no longer any sea"* (Rev. 21:1). The careful reader will notice that the new heaven and the new earth will come down out of heaven from God (Rev. 21:2). Clearly this text suggests that in order to experience the pleasures of heaven one must not go "up," but receive and enter that which is coming down.

Previously I referred to songs that teach poor theology. Recently however I listened to a song that actually champions the word of God rather than concocting an idea that fits one's thinking. The song is entitled, "The City That's Coming Down." The lyrics of this song speak loudly against the thought that we must go up to experience the "new Jerusalem." Obviously the writer of this song has read Revelation 21 and knew that the holy city would be coming down (Rev. 21:2).

It is in this passage that we discover for certain that those who die are not with God immediately upon their death. God's declaration following the descent of the New Jerusalem confirms this truth, "*Now the dwelling of God is with men, and he will live with them. They will be his people, and God himself will be with them and be their God*" (Rev. 21:3). If only now God dwells with man how can man be with him already?

John paints this event in terms of a wedding where the bride is coming down the isle to see the groom for the first time. In most weddings, the groom is not permitted nor does he desire to see the bride prior to the wedding ceremony itself. It is at this juncture that we realize that the holy city of New Jerusalem will be coming down in the same way a bride walks down the isle to meet her groom. It is at this time that God will "*wipe every tear from their eyes*" (Rev. 21:4). In the New Jerusalem "*there will be no more death or mourning or crying or pain for the old order of things has passed away*" (Rev. 21:4).

IT'S ALL IN THE TIMING

Perhaps one of the greatest biblical passages is attributed to Paul in 1 Corinthians 15. Most people affectionately call it the "resurrection" chapter and one only needs to read it once to know why. In this passage Paul reveals that everything hinges on the resurrection. Everything, especially our future, depends on whether or not Christ was raised from the dead. If he was raised (and Paul emphatically states that he was), then we have hope for the future.

If Christ has been raised then there is hope for those who have fallen asleep (1 Cor. 15:18) because if all we have to hope for is this life then we are to be pitied above all men (1 Cor. 15:19). Since Christ was raised and seen by Paul himself, we can look forward to that day when Christ will return and everything will be changed (1 Cor. 15:51). No longer will we be confined to the grave and the dust to which we have returned. That which died temporarily will rise up to experience eternal life for Paul states that the perishable will inherit the imperishable (1 Cor. 15:50) and the mortal will be clothed with immortality (1 Cor. 15:53). As all died in Adam (1 Cor. 15:22) all in Christ will be made alive (1 Cor. 15:22) but each in his own turn: Christ, the firstfruits; then, when he comes, those who belong to him.

It is at this point that Paul says the end will come (1 Cor. 15:24). When this happens, it will also spell the end for death. Finally death will be "*swallowed up in victory*" (1 Cor. 15:54). Until then, death will continue to seemingly have the upper hand, wreaking havoc on mankind but according to God's plan its end will come.

Notice if you will the timing of this event. Death is not eliminated until the second coming, the same time at which man is changed from a mortal and perishable being into an immortal and nonperishable being. This is the same time that God will destroy the old heavens and earth in order to bring down the city of New Jerusalem to be the dwelling place for God and his people.

It is also the time at which all heartache and sorrow will be done away with. This will happen at the time when the new heavens and new earth have been established and the old ones have been destroyed by fire. Since the old ones have not experienced their own destruction yet we can safely discern that the new ones are still under construction (John 14:1–4). Since the new ones are brought into being at the time of the destruction of the old we can also determine that they are not inhabited by people now.

A FINAL WORD

Years ago we used to sing the familiar tune, "Heaven is a wonderful place, filled with glory and grace. I want to see my Savior's face, heaven is a wonderful, very, very wonderful; heaven is a wonderful place. But, until then my heart will go on singing."

Knowing that God has prepared a place for me that "*no eye has seen, no ear has heard, no mind has conceived*" (1 Cor. 2:9) brings excitement to my heart and mind. I look forward to the day when I will enter his presence, along with Noah, David, Abraham, Isaac, and countless others who are now waiting for the Lord's return (Heb. 11:39–40). Together at the second coming we will inherit the kingdom of heaven (Matt. 5:3–10) and live with the Lord forever more. There are many things one may choose to believe about heaven and the establishment of God's kingdom, both on this earth and in the world to come, but there is only one true picture of what will happen on that day. The bottom line has been drawn by the hand of God in his word. It is by God's own words a trustworthy and true statement of what will take place (Rev. 21:5). The question is whether or not we are going to believe the predominant teaching of his word or cling to thinking of the day?

God has not promised that we would be with him immediately after dying but he has committed himself to redeeming us to an eternal relationship when he establishes his kingdom at the time of the second coming and resurrection. With him, we have hope; without him, we will be lost forever.

There is nothing in us inherently that will guarantee our continued existence in any sense for he is God and we are human. He is immortal and we are mortal. He lives forever but without him we will perish. He will return in the person of Christ to claim those who believe in his Son. He will come back and carry out the resurrection. We will inherit the kingdom of heaven but not until then. We will live forever, but not until then. We will see the end of death, mourning, and sorrow but not until then. We will dwell with God and see him as he is but not until then. *Not, until then.*

16

On One Condition

*"The best reply to an atheist is to give him a dinner and ask him if he believes
there is a chef who prepared it."*

—Anonymous

Family traditions are special. One that has stuck in the Warren family is the singing of what my dad called "ditties." You know what I mean. Ditties are those silly
little songs or sayings that have a way of becoming part of a family down through
the years.

My grandfather was a "ditty" singer. I can still remember him putting me on
his lap and while grasping both of my wrists having me try to clap my hands as he
sang to me the "thumpytom" song. That was my personal ditty and I will never
forget it.

I'm a ditty singer too and so is my oldest son. Our house is filled with those
songs that mean everything to us but would cause others to think that we have
lost our minds. No one escapes a ditty, even our animals. Ditties are personal
expressions of truth. It's the way we let each other know that we really love each
other. When you are the brunt of a ditty, you are really loved.

TO THE END OF THE COUNT

While my oldest son gravitated toward the singing of ditties, my youngest boy
was fond of those affectionate sayings that are often heard between a father and
his son. Of all the sayings, one stands out in my memory. It was coined one night
as I put my son to bed. Before turning out the light I told him "I love you!" He
responded by asking me the question, "How much do you love me Daddy?" Not
knowing exactly what I should say, I blurted out the first thing that came to my
mind. To an adult it probably wouldn't make sense but for a four year old it
worked. I simply said, *"to the end of the count."* And then I explained to my son

that for me there was no end of the count meaning that I loved him with an everlasting love, one that will never run out. Through these simple words we connected.

THE LANGUAGE OF LOVE

In John's gospel, which contains some of the most beautiful words ever expressed to mankind, we discover how God the Father connected through Christ with a sinful world. In John 1:14, John reveals, "*The Word (logos) became flesh and made his dwelling among us. We have seen his glory, the glory of the One and only, full of grace and truth.*" Here we can see how much God the Father loved us. He loved us so much that he sent his very best. In chapter three we find out just how far God was willing to take this expression of love, by declaring that he "*so loved the world that he gave his one and only Son, that whoever believes in him shall not perish but have everlasting life*" (John 3:16).

God's greatest expression of love clearly demonstrates what it means to love someone to the end of the count. God was not willing for anyone to be excluded from his love knowing that they would perish without it.

RESCUE THE PERISHING

I can still remember singing the words of the old hymn, which included, "Rescue the Perishing, Care for the Dying." The idea that a person needs to be rescued from perishing suggests that if one is not rescued, he or she will perish. I have often thought, "If people don't perish, what's the need for a rescue?" Even more, "If people don't perish, why would God send his Son to die for them?" (John 3:16).

The thought that one has nothing to fear in light of God's prediction of death in the Garden of Eden has corrupted the true biblical view of redemption throughout history. Such a theology, which expresses the idea that mankind is not mortal and therefore he will not perish, is common today. An important part of this discussion is that God so loved the world in order that no one would *perish*, provided they accepted by faith the redemptive work of Christ on the cross and his resurrection from the dead (Rom. 10:9–13). The conclusion therefore is that if a person refuses the work of Christ on his or her behalf they will die (Heb. 9:27) and ultimately perish in the end. This being true John's words in 1 John 5:11–12 ring loud and clear, "*God has given us eternal life, and this life is in his Son. He who has the Son has life; he who does not have the Son of God does not have life.*" If man cannot have life apart from a relationship with Christ he does not have life within himself. He cannot be inherently immortal.

The belief in the eternal nature of man has long been considered a given theologically even though the Bible itself does not specifically address or confirm the belief. This belief is popular, even though terms such as "immortal soul," "disembodied soul," "intermediate state," "eternal soul," "eternal conscious torment," "purgatory," or "eternal separation from God" are never mentioned in the pages of the Bible. On the contrary, man is seen as one who is subject to death or, in other words, mortal.

According to the Scriptures, death is described as a condition of silence (Eccles. 9:5–6, 10), decay (Ps. 49:12, 14), hopelessness (Job 14:7–12), the absence of praise (Ps. 88:11–12), and a lack of memory (Ps. 6:4–5). When one sees in the Scripture that man is so completely dissolved and disabled by death it is logical to conclude that he cannot be inherently immortal. Throughout the pages of the Bible, man is described as one who receives the gift of eternal life due to his faith in Christ (Rom. 6:23), and one who *seeks after* immortality (Rom. 2:7). If man seeks after immortality, how can he possess it naturally? Why would one need that which he already possesses? On the other hand, Paul's understanding of the gospel (Rom. 2:16, 1 Cor. 15:53) reveals that the reception of this immortal gift will take place at the second coming on the day when God will judge men's secrets through Jesus Christ (Rom. 2:16).

WHO IS LIKE OUR GOD?

God on the other hand is seen as the only one who has intrinsic immortality. Paul speaks about the nature of God in his first letter to Timothy as he considers his own unworthiness to receive the gospel. He describes his feelings in this way, "*Here is a trustworthy saying that deserves full acceptance: Christ Jesus came into the world to save sinners—of whom I am the worst, but for that very reason I was shown mercy so that in me, the worst of sinners, Christ Jesus might display his unlimited patience as an example for those who would believe on him and receive eternal life*" (1 Tim. 1:15–17).

The very idea that Paul describes himself in this way argues strongly for the belief that he is not equal to God on any level. Realizing that he did not deserve the gift of eternal life Paul breaks out in a verbal benediction of praise; acknowledging God as "*eternal, immortal, invisible, the only God.*" (1 Tim. 1:17). These characteristics of God are elaborated upon by Paul in the concluding words of his first letter (1 Tim. 6:16). In an attempt to encourage Timothy to be faithful to

God's call upon his life, Paul draws upon the faithful and trustworthy nature of God who will hold him accountable at the *"appearing of our Lord Jesus Christ"* (1 Tim. 6:14), a time that *"God, the blessed and only Ruler, the King of Kings and Lord of lords, who alone is immortal and who lives in unapproachable light, whom no one has seen or can see"* will determine in his own time (1 Tim. 6:16).

Paul's description of God's nature testifies that there is no one like his God. According to Paul, God *alone* is immortal. Taken at face value, this means that God is the only one who is immortal and since he alone is immortal we must conclude that no one else is. This has tremendous implications for those who profess that man is an immortal being and is not bound by death nor will he perish. Even if one concedes that man is immortal one would be hard pressed to remove the reception of this gift from the time of the second coming of Christ as only then will the mortal become immortal (1 Cor. 15:52–54).

GOD ALONE

The theology of man that accepts the immortality of the soul prior to the second coming must by-pass the clear teaching of 1 Timothy 6:16 which states without confusion that God *alone* is immortal. Fortunately this is not the only place in the New Testament where God is described as the one with an attribute that He alone possesses.

A PICTURE OF GOD

The crowd was pressing around Jesus when some men brought a paralytic to him in an attempt to get him healed. They went so far as to cut a hole in the roof in order to lower him down to Jesus. The evidence of their faith caused Jesus to heal the man and prompted a severe criticism from the local teachers of the law arguing not against the action of Jesus but the underlying message of his words. That Jesus equated himself with God led to shouts of blasphemy and an attempt to draw a distinction between man and God, a distinction that was heard in their cry, *"Who can forgive sins but God alone?"* (Mark 2:7).

Over and over again the Bible presents God as one who continually reaches out to sinful man, despite the belief that his character far exceeds that of mankind. God alone is holy (Rev. 15:4), good, and perfect in nature, yet constantly pictured as the one who seeks after man in order to restore the relationship that was broken in the Garden of Eden. Time and time again God's plan to restore mankind into a right relationship with his maker is presented in a "conditional" manner. If the condition is met, then God will keep his word according to his promises. If the condition is not met, then God will also keep his word according to his promises.

ON ONE CONDITION

The conditional nature of God's promises to man makes sense in view of God's inapproachability. Paul reminded young Timothy that God "*lives in unapproachable light, whom no one has seen or can see*" (1 Tim. 6:16). In the words of John the apostle (John 1:18), the only one who has ever seen God the Father is "*God the One and only,*" whom according to John 1:14 is the word or the Son of God. Based on the context the Word is clearly Jesus Christ.

If God is unapproachable in his nature, and Christ is the only one who has seen him, how can one think that mankind has full access to his presence at the point of death when the Bible is clear that man will not possess a body that is fit for the kingdom of God where God dwells until he receives it at the time of the second coming (1 Cor. 15:49)? Meanwhile, nothing has changed from the time of Moses when God had to protect him from being exposed to God's full presence (Exod. 33:21) due to the fact that no one can see God and live (Exod. 33:20).

In the New Testament God's nature was visible in Christ as revealed in Jesus's words to Philip when he told him, "*anyone who has seen me has seen the Father*" (John 14:9). For John, Jesus was the perfect picture of God's glory, "*the glory of the One and only, who came from the Father, full of grace and truth*" (John 1:14). Until Christ returns, he will be the only one that can see the Father but "*We know that when he appears, we shall be like him, for we shall see him as he is*" (1 John 3:2).

This being true one might find it difficult to explain how a person can be in paradise or heaven at the point of death and in the presence of God when according to the Bible no one who is mortal can do this and live. John clearly writes that we will only see God when He comes and only then will we be like him. How then can a person experience this level of a relationship with an eternal God when he is a mere mortal? The answer is found in the resurrection, his and ours.

WHEN HE COMES

Since man is not inherently immortal, a truth revealed throughout the Bible, and not to be viewed as one who is taken apart at death (disembodied) allowing the soul and spirit to separate from the body in order to experience an immediate presence with the Lord *what is God's plan for mortal man?*

One thing is for certain since man is mortal. The second coming of Christ will not be a time when man is simply "re-embodied" by the putting back together of the parts that were "disembodied" at the point of death. Rather, according to Paul the resurrection will be the time when the mortal will experience a change into that which is immortal (1 Cor. 15:51–54). Until that time man will return to the dust of the ground, a fate reserved for everyone (Eccles. 12:7), and await the voice of the Son of God (John 5:25), who on the last day will call them out of the grave (John 6:39–40, 43–44) to be forever with the Lord (1 Thess. 4:13–17).

The resurrection is the key for mankind if he ever hopes to be reunited with Christ. In his classic chapter on this theme Paul makes it clear that if Christ was not raised from the dead, *"Then those who have fallen asleep [died] in Christ are lost"* (1 Cor. 15:18). If Christ has not been raised then those who are still in their graves are lost and will never be raised. Only because Christ was the firstfruits of those who have died and come back to life (1 Cor. 15:20) will the entire harvest of believers who have put their faith in him be raised when he returns (1 Cor. 15:18–19). Until then, though our citizenship is in heaven, we eagerly await a Savior from there (Phil. 3:20), and make residence here on earth, *"while we wait for the glorious appearing of our great God and Savior, Jesus Christ"* (Titus 2:13).

This biblical view has a definite impact on the way one views death and life. Because man is mortal the Bible says that he will not live forever unless he is in relationship with the one who is immortal and is the imparter of this gift. Man's eternal future is conditional. If by faith he enters into a relationship with Christ he will live again proving true the Proverbial saying, *"in the way of righteousness there is life; along that path is immortality"* (Prov. 12:28). If not he is without hope and *"to be pitied more than all men"* (1 Cor. 15:19b).

What then does the future hold for those without Christ? Can a mortal live forever in the presence of the immortal God without the gift of immortality? If not, what happens to mortal man when he faces the judgment of God? Will he live forever or will his life come to an end? That is the final question.

17

Life Only in Christ!

"Nothing will ever be accomplished if every objection must be overcome."

—Samuel Johnson

In the beginning of this study, I asked you to join me on a journey through the Bible in a search for truth. While we have examined a lot of texts and considered many subjects, our goal has been to allow the text to speak for itself and our purpose was to seek the truth no matter how different it might be from what we already believe. In many cases it has been suggested, even argued, that the text does not match the prevalent teaching found so often in the Christian community today. Now at the conclusion of this study, we are brought to a point of decision. Specifically, does the biblical evidence speak to a view of the truth that we have not seen before and, if so, will we believe it?

In the spirit of baseball legend Yogi Berra, who said, "You can observe a lot by watching," our investigation of God's word has shown that one can "learn a lot by thinking." Theological concepts exist today and are readily accepted without biblical justification arguing strongly for the idea that many people have thought about real issues, but have failed to learn anything regarding what the Bible actually teaches on these subjects.

THE STATE OF THE CHURCH

One might wonder exactly how the church could reach the point where it accepts a particular view of Scripture especially as it pertains to the nature of man and his destiny with or without Christ when there is such an overwhelming source of evidence suggesting an alternate position to that which is commonly believed. When the Bible states that man is "*mortal*," how did he become an *immortal* being who is on an equal plane with his creator? When man was created as a whole person and brought to life by the breath of God, how did he become a spiritual being that experiences a kind of Platonic escapism at death without biblical support?

Having a distorted view of man's nature has led to a variety of theological positions that are unwarranted by the Scriptures. Since man is seen as a "spiritual" being, death is presented by most as the time when the real man "flies away" to experience an immortal existence either in heaven or in hell, despite man being mortal and by definition unable to live forever. Heaven has become a mystical place beyond the clouds and stars where the inner man goes immediately upon his death. In this interpretation, death ceases to be death and becomes the doorway to another world. Death is no longer seen as the great enemy spoken of by Paul in 1 Corinthians, but becomes the friend of all mankind. This view however contradicts the statements presented by Paul that death will be the last great enemy destroyed by God at the time of the resurrection.

The problem with this entire outlook is that, according to Jesus's own words (John 14:1–4), he left this world in order to go and prepare for a new heaven and earth that will be created by the time he comes back to get his bride (Rev. 21:1–4). It is hard to imagine how those who die can be with Jesus when he has yet to return to claim them.

WHAT TIME IS IT?

Two thousand years have passed since Jesus, his disciples, and countless other followers of Christ first lived on earth and sought to carry out the work of Christ throughout the known world. One might be surprised to discover that in only a few years the church was already battling the presence of heresy within its ranks. Unfortunately times have changed little since that day.

The presence of false teaching is not surprising given the fallen nature of man and our propensity for doing things our own way. Paul was mindful of this probability when he told the believers in Ephesus that there would come a time when "*men will not put up with sound doctrine. Instead, to suit their own desires, they will gather around them a great number of teachers to say what their itching ears want to hear. They will turn their ears away from the truth and turn aside to myths*" (2 Tim. 4:3–4). It is the conviction of the author that much of the thinking present in the church today pertaining to man's nature and his eternal destiny represents such a turn away from the truth.

IN THE MINORITY

During the past thirty years, I have noticed an amazing tendency among those who hold to the traditional view on subjects like man's nature and destiny especially as it pertains to ideas about heaven and hell. Those who hold these views have little if any understanding of other views regarding the subject at hand. In fact, what they do believe is quite often a regurgitation of what they have been forced fed by pastors and teachers throughout their entire life. Sadly, this is also true for those who believe in the view presented in this book, known as the "conditionalist" position. The presence of such biblical illiteracy suggests a violation of Paul's admonition for Timothy to be a person who *"correctly handles the word of truth"* (2 Tim. 2:15b).

THE SIMPLE TRUTH

As I have contended from the beginning, the Bible is not that hard to understand. The problem comes when we jump to premature conclusions about the teaching of any subject in the Bible. If we are not careful, we will find ourselves holding convictions that are totally unwarranted in light of the Scriptures and unable to hold up under the scrutiny of careful exegesis.

The writer of the Proverbs once said, *"It is not good to have zeal without knowledge, nor to be hasty and miss the way"* (Prov. 19:2). While God would not want us to lay hands on a leader prematurely, he also desires that we not endorse a particular teaching of the Bible too quickly without allowing the evidence to speak for itself. This must include our willingness to let the Scripture interpret Scripture and avoid all attempts of eisegesis (reading our thoughts into the text). When faced with a decision regarding the meaning of a text, we must make a choice not based on our personal preference but on the whole counsel of God found in the word of God and nowhere else.

Once again, allow me to quote that great philosopher of the twentieth century, Yogi Berra, when he said, *"When you come to a fork in the road, take it."* I can't imagine someone reading the discussion presented in this book and not finding themselves at a fork in the road on the theological map of their lives. The question is: "Which way will you go?"

LIFE ONLY IN CHRIST

Apart from determining the Bible's position on man's nature and his destiny, there is a more fundamental and foundational question that must be answered by the diligent student of God's word. It is the question of whether or not we are willing to allow God to be God.

Nowhere in the Bible is man presented as being immortal prior to the second coming. Nowhere is he seen as being equal with God in the nature of his being. From the beginning of the Bible to the end, God is the creator and sustainer of man's life. Man is pictured as being a mortal being and without God man would be lost and unable to exist. It is a fanciful thought to proclaim that we possess within our being the ability to exist forever without the capability to do so being given to us. When the Bible says, *"God alone is immortal"* (1 Tim. 6:16) one must decide, "Is it true or not?"

John 3:16, the most popular and well-known verse in the entire Bible, speaks to the reason God sent Christ into the world to redeem mankind. Contrary to popular belief, God was the first "purpose driven" being as he sent his Son to insure that those who believed in him would not perish. The concept of perishing includes the understanding that whatever perishes ceases to exist. The simple conclusion for John would be that anyone who does not believe in Christ will perish. Anyone who does not have a personal relationship with Christ in the end will cease to exist or perish. Christ came to prevent this but it will be the result for those who choose not to believe. The idea of "life only in Christ" is presented in no uncertain terms by John in his epistle declaring, *"He who has the Son has life; he who does not have the Son of God does not have life"* (1 John 5:12). In a nutshell, this is the essence of eternal life (1 John 5:11).

The idea that man has immortality apart from Christ giving it to him at the time of the resurrection is the height of spiritual arrogance. If true this would mean that man has found some way to be like God without God making it possible and have no real need for him. However the Bible says that it is only at the second coming when the mortal will become immortal and the perishable will become imperishable (1 Cor. 15:53) and finally be like him (1 John 3:2).

While death is applicable to everyone life eternal or immortality at the second coming is waiting for those who call Jesus Lord. On that glorious day we will be changed from a mortal, having to experience death as a result of our sin type being, into an immortal person who has been given the gift of eternal life.

I cannot help but think about what a day that will be. We will join together with loved ones who have died years ago and we will meet for the very first time saints of old that we have read about in the Bible since we were young children.

We will walk and talk with Jesus, *"the author and perfector of our faith"* (Heb. 12:2). All of our trials and struggles in this life will fade into insignificance because of him. We will sing to the top of our voices, praise flowing from our hearts knowing that it was worth it all. We will know that we fought the fight, kept the faith, and finished the race not because of our own power, but because of him. We will rejoice when we receive our *"crown of righteousness"* (2 Tim. 4:8) on that day and be elated to share it with *"all who have longed for his appearing"* (2 Tim. 4:8).

One is hard pressed to read the Bible and think that man is the center of everything. Clearly, God is central. Like a mother who gives life to her child, God gives life to his children. We exist because he does. We have hope because he provides it. Our life both here and in the future depends on God's grace. Life only in Christ is more than a snappy slogan. It is the nucleus of our belief around which all other things revolve. Life only in Christ is the heart of our message for a world lost in sin. It is the life preserver that must be thrown to those without Christ and in need of rescue. Life only in Christ is the one thing that provides hope for a dying world, one that will perish without him. In the words of that familiar song, we must "Rescue the perishing, duty demands it." We must unashamedly take the message of a Savior that cares and a Savior that saves to the world for physical and spiritual life both in this world and in the world to come is found only in him.

Epilogue

"It takes two to speak the truth—one to speak and another to hear."

—Henry David Thoreau

There has long been debate as to which is the speedier, truth or error; which spreads faster, false report or denial. Some have maintained that truth has sturdier and surer wings. Others contend that fiction and careless rumor find more willing tongues to speed them on their way. Long ago, Tacitus, the Roman historian, gave his judgment in these words: *"Truth is confirmed by inspection and delay: falsehood by haste and uncertainty."*[1]

I am hopeful that now that our journey is over you have not only enjoyed our inspection of God's word regarding the nature of man and his eternal destiny but that you have gained an appreciation and respect for the unity of God's word and its message to mankind.

Throughout this examination of the Bible we have seen that when it comes to man and God there is a clear difference. God is pictured as the eternal, always existing creator of mankind and the only one who inherently possesses the attribute of immortality. On the other hand mankind is God's greatest creation who was a candidate for immortality in the beginning but forfeited this gift due to sin. Man is mortal and can become immortal only by receiving the gift of immortality at the end of time as we know it.

Man's mortality argues for at least three realities for the future. First, man will die and because he is mortal the only way he will experience life beyond death will be due to the belief that God himself will call him from the grave at the time of the second coming (1 Corinthians 15). Secondly, because man is mortal and does not possess immortality as an inherent attribute of his nature it will be given to him when Christ returns provided he has placed his faith in him for the salvation of his soul. Finally, the fact that mankind is mortal demands that he will not continue to live apart from Christ living in him through faith. This means that mankind will cease to exist following the judgment. Only those who place their faith in Christ will continue to live eternally. All others will perish.

Now that you have completed the reading of this book what do you think? Is it conceivable that what you have believed all of your life has not been correct?

The study provided in this work has certainly raised some very important issues regarding this question.

CONCLUDING REMARKS

Truth is confirmed by inspection. Has this been true for you? Have you seen enough evidence in this work to reconsider your thoughts concerning man's nature? Are you willing to rethink your concept of hell? If what you've read in this book sounds convincing, what will it take for you to change your mind?

My prayer is that you have been challenged by the content of this book and that somehow your life has been blessed. The primary purpose of this work was to search for the truth, even if it demanded that I change my mind. The end result was exactly the opposite. While I have learned many things throughout this adventure of exploring God's word, my thoughts have been confirmed regarding the nature of God and man. God truly is our source of strength, but, even more, he is our source of life. The Scriptures put it this way: "*The God who made the world and everything in it is the Lord of heaven and earth and does not live in temples built by hands. And he is not served by human hands, as if he needed anything, because he himself gives all men life and breath and everything else. From one man he made every nation of men that they should inhabit the whole earth; and he determined the times set for them and the exact places where they should live. God did this so that men would seek him and perhaps reach out for him and find him, though he is not far from each one of us. For in him we live and move and have our being*" (Acts 17:24–28a).

APPENDIX A

Problematic Passages

Occasionally you read the Bible and come across texts that do not seem to agree with your overall understanding of the Bible's broader teaching on a given subject. This is certainly true for those who believe in the natural mortality of man over against the idea that man inherently possesses immortality. Below, you will find a few of those problematic passages that must not be overlooked.

The following commentary on these selected passages is not intended to be the final word on how these texts should be interpreted, but an attempt to show how they can be understood within the broader teaching of the Bible on the mortal nature of man and his eternal destiny.

The Witch at Endor (1 Samuel 28:1–25)

There are those who suggest that the result of King Saul's consulting the witch at Endor lends evidence to the belief that people enter heaven or hell upon their death. However, after a closer look at the text itself, one is able to discern a lack of evidence for such a position.

The context is one of battle. King Saul and the army of Israel were confronted by the Philistines. Saul's heart was filled with fear and gripped by terror (1 Sam. 28:6) to the degree that He sought the direction of the Lord. Unfortunately for Saul, the Lord did not answer him (1 Sam. 28:6). Saul became so desperate for an answer that he told his servants to seek out the help of a medium, so he could inquire an answer to his problem. This is an interesting action on the part of Saul, since the text says that Saul had expelled the mediums and spiritists from the land (1 Sam. 28:3). Supposedly, Saul did this in view of the Levitical law (Lev. 19:26).

That this was not an action that pleased God was demonstrated in the way Saul went about getting the information. The first thing he did was to disguise himself so the witch of Endor could not recognize him. I find it very interesting that the king who was willing to deceive was seeking the truth. Wearing this disguise, he asked her to consult a spirit for him and said, *"bring up for me the one I name"* (1 Sam. 28:8).

It is interesting to see the woman's reaction when she saw a spirit resembling Samuel. Immediately, upon seeing the spirit, she was able to recognize Saul and was afraid for her life. After Saul assured her that she would be okay, he continued to ask her what she saw. Of course, she saw a spirit that looked like Samuel. King Saul prostrated himself before Samuel in an attempt to get his help.

According to the text, Samuel is not particularly thrilled that Saul has bothered him. Saul admits that God had not answered him regarding this matter and that this is the reason that he has sought his counsel (1 Sam. 28:15). Samuel asked Saul why he had disturbed him by bringing him up (1 Sam. 28:15). That Samuel considered his being brought "up" as a disturbance suggests that this is not a normal activity and not necessarily one that should happen.

King Saul makes it clear that he has called upon Samuel because God had not responded. Upon hearing this, Samuel simply reiterates what Saul already knew concerning his disobedience and the promised results of that disobedience (1 Sam. 28:17–18). Further, Samuel makes it clear that Saul and the Israelites would fall and that he would die and join Samuel tomorrow (1 Sam. 28:19). Obviously, Saul did not receive the kind of news that he was hoping for when he consulted the medium. Rather than learning about his victory, Saul discovered that he would not only lose the battle, but his life (1 Sam. 15:26, 28).

The first thing one recognizes about this text is that it is not written to teach us about heaven or hell. That is not its purpose. This is a text about disobedience and deception. It is about King Saul trying to bypass the word of the Lord, and find a way to get his way. It's about trying to find any means to get what you want, even if that means talking to the spirits.

There is nothing in this text or the rest of the Bible that suggests that people exist in the ground as spirits and can be conjured up through a séance for help. Samuel himself implies by his own words that what was happening was irregular and unexpected (1 Sam. 28:15).

It is very unlikely that this text is intended to be used as a guide for our understanding on what happens when people die. The text is clearly speaking about an occurrence that is not the norm. Therefore, it is safe to assume that this text provides no reasonable explanation for what happens when one dies. That the Old Testament rejected the use of mediums and spiritists, and that King Saul had removed them from the land of the kingdom, argues strongly for the belief that God did not approve of their use, or the adoption of what they say. In essence, they were seen as being evil and standing in direct opposition to the work of the Spirit of God. It hardly seems probable that God would endorse what they do, much less what they say. However, truth is truth and in spite of King Saul's end run around the Lord, God allowed this spirit to speak the truth about what was going to happen to Saul and Israel.

In conclusion, we must note that Saul never actually saw Samuel, but communicated with Samuel through the lady at Endor. In 1 Samuel 27:21, the text suggests that the woman came to Saul after she was finished serving as a medium with Samuel. In regards to Samuel's actual appearance, there is enough evidence in the text to indicate that Samuel didn't actually have a body (*"I see a spirit coming out of the ground"*) (1 Sam. 27:13), yet somehow he appeared to have clothes (wearing a robe). The specifics of the text seem to suggest that this was more like a vision, than an actual bodily appearance of Samuel.

This was not a resurrection event, therefore it is likely that God was not a part of this event, apart from the passages demonstrating that he allowed this vision/ appearance of Samuel to communicate the truth to Saul which it turns out he already knew. In actuality, Saul didn't even need a medium, as he already knew what would happen to him, as it had been prophesied.

The Transfiguration (Matthew 17:1–13)

At first glance, this passage may seem to indicate that Moses and Elijah are alive even though Moses was dead and Elijah had been taken from this life. The transfiguration, however, is not intended to reveal an actual occurrence, but is more likely a vision similar to that experienced by Peter in Acts 11:5–10.

The same Greek word, (Grk. *orama*), is used to describe the action in each scene (Matt. 17:9; Acts 11:5). In each passage, the disciples were said to have "seen" something. In Matthew, Peter and James saw Jesus, along with Moses and Elijah. In the book of Acts, Peter saw a vision of a sheet and wild animals coming down from heaven.

Since the Bible teaches that man is mortal and will not live beyond the grave until Christ returns a second time, this must be a vision. If this is true, what bodies would these be since the bodily resurrection has not yet taken place? The resurrection of the believers, among which we would find Moses and Elijah, has not yet taken place.

In 1 Corinthians 15:22–23, we read that Christ was destined to die and become the firstfruits of those who have already experienced death by coming out of the grave. Clearly, Christ was to be the first person clothed with a body fit for the kingdom of God. No one was to precede him in this process (1 Cor. 15:23). If this weren't enough, Acts 16:9 and Acts 18:9 suggest that when the word *orama* is used, at least by Luke, the idea of what is seen in a vision is on his mind.

The Resurrection Question (Matthew 22:23–33)

The general context of this passage is one in which the Pharisees and the Sadducees are attempting to trap Jesus in his own teaching (Matt. 22:15, 23). The question coming from the Sadducees regarding marriage appears to be asked in mockery when a lady begins to asks, "*Now then, at the resurrection...*" (Matt. 22:28). This is significant since the Sadducees were known for their disbelief in the resurrection (1 Cor. 15:23).

Some might think that Jesus was defending the idea that Abraham, Isaac, and Jacob were alive at that very moment when he said, "*He is not the God of the dead but of the living*" (Matt. 22:32). However, in saying this, Jesus was actually supporting the idea of the resurrection, which they did not believe. By stating that God was the God of the living, he was declaring that the resurrection of the dead is a reality. That is, that the dead would not remain dead but arise and live. Jesus was teaching that Abraham, Isaac, and Jacob will live again because God is the God of the living and they will not be living again until the time of the resurrection.

One important aspect of Jesus's teaching here is worthy of special notice. If the spiritual fathers (Abraham, Isaac, and Jacob) are living right now, as some believe, how does this passage prove that the resurrection is real? Rather than teaching that these spiritual giants are alive right now, this passage teaches that the resurrection is the means by which Abraham, Isaac, and Jacob will live again.

Holy People Were Raised to Life at Jesus's Resurrection (Matthew 27:50–54)

Many have wondered about the meaning and significance of the resurrection of people from the dead at the time of Christ's death on the cross. A closer examination of this text reveals some interesting insights.

Matthew tells us that when Christ died on the cross that many holy people were raised from the dead as their tombs broke open during the earthquake, which occurred at the time of the crucifixion (Matt. 27:54). It is worth noting that not everyone was raised, but many. And, not just anyone was raised but many "holy" people. Obviously, this suggests that the people raised from the dead were noticeably people from the religious sector of the society.

Since we know that the general resurrection of the dead will take place at the second coming of Christ (1 Cor. 15), this happening was a one-time event and occurred for a reason. We may find in Matthew 27:53 the answer to the question, "Why did the holy people who were raised from the dead go into town and appear to many people?" Given the religious environment of Jesus's day, there is one thing that would definitely make a difference to the naysayers in town, especially all of the religious people who had rejected Christ and his claims to deity. What could be more convincing than to see holy people, whom they had known, come walking into town?

The text suggests that being raised from the dead was specifically tied to the resurrection of Christ from the dead three days later (Matt. 27:53). It is worth noting that there is no evidence from this text or reason to believe based on this text that the resurrection experience of the holy people in this text is any different than the resurrection experience of a person like Lazarus. They were not raised in the same way as they will be at the second coming. These holy people, like Lazarus, were raised, only to die again.

If the resurrection (1 Cor. 15) is not a reembodiment (death perceived as a disembodiment or separation of a body and soul) but a change (as taught in 1 Cor. 15) from one thing into another (earthly body into a heavenly body fit for the kingdom), then the holy people raised at this time were simply people who had the breath of life put back into them, like Lazarus, and they lived again. Unfortunately, they would also die again.

In the end, the purpose and significance of this text is to show the connection of Christ's death, burial, and resurrection to the possibility of resurrection for anyone. It would seem most probable that the reason the people went into town following the resurrection of Christ was to demonstrate his power over death. They did not go into town to talk about how great heaven was (presumably this is where most would think that they were residing) but to declare visibly the power of Christ over death.

The culture of the first century was very "religious" but not very accepting to the Messiah claims of Christ, the one they had just crucified. It is quite interesting to at least ponder whether or not the holy people, who were raised from the dead, gave their lives to Christ in faith following this unbelievable happening in their lives. For this is the real reason for this text, to show that Jesus really is the resurrection and the life.

Enoch: Taken from This Life (Hebrews 11:5)

There are some who suggest that Enoch was taken from this life directly into heaven. If this was true, it would mean that Enoch entered heaven prior to Christ. If this is true, it would be extremely difficult, if not impossible, to understand this passage in light of John 3:13 which states, *"No one has ever gone into heaven except the one who came from heaven—the Son of Man."*

In light of 1 Timothy 6:16, it would appear that the apostle Paul agrees. Apparently, no one has seen the Father except God the Son (John 1:18), because he lives in unapproachable light; nor can anyone see him. This would mean that Enoch has not seen him either.

Some have tried to equate the idea of being transformed with the change that will take place at the time of the resurrection. However, this would mean that Enoch experienced the body fit for the kingdom prior to Jesus. This would violate the belief that Christ has preeminence *"in all things"* (Colossians 1:18).

Others have suggested that Enoch is simply in holding, while some argue that Enoch eventually died in light of Hebrews 11:13. Whatever scenario might be imagined, it seems very improbable that Enoch received an immortal body prior to Christ by going to "heaven."

Preaching to the Spirits (1 Peter 3:18–20)

There are those who suggest that this text teaches that there is a hell containing the ungodly "eternal spirits" of men. Based on this text and 2 Peter 2:4–5 it makes more sense to believe that Peter is referring to angels in 1 Peter 3:18–20.

Since angels are spirit beings, it makes sense that they are the "spirits' in prison. Besides, here and here alone do we see the use of the word *tartarosas*[1] for hell (2 Peter 2:4). The word is neither Hades nor Gehenna, which are commonly used in the New Testament. When Jesus speaks of hell, he always uses the word *Gehenna* in relationship to judgment. The single use of the word *tartarosas* argues strongly for its relationship with angels rather than man. Christ preaching to them is probably best understood to mean something like making a proclamation, since the word used is *kerusso* (proclaim).

In the New Testament, two Greek words are translated "preach." One is *euanggelizo*, "to announce good news." It is usually translated "preach the gospel" or "preach the good news" in the NIV and NASB. The other word is *kerusso*, which means "to proclaim, or to announce publicly."

Many have seen this angelic attack as an attempt to stop the lineage through which Jesus would come. Therefore, it makes sense that Jesus would go and proclaim (Grk. *kerusso*) to them that his work was finished. He went to tell them that He had won despite their efforts to ruin His plan.

The Fifth Seal: Souls Under the Altar (Revelation 6:9–11)

At first glance, this passage might seem to suggest that God is holding eternal souls under the altar until the end of the age. However, what at first appears to be literal is most likely figurative language that gives a voice to those who have died.

It has been suggested that this language is not that different than the words used by God in speaking to Cain when he said, "*Your brother's blood cries out to me from the ground*" (Gen. 4:10). In the same way, the testimonies and souls of the ones who have died cried out in a loud voice (Rev. 6:9–10).

While this passage may appear to suggest a literal crying out from souls that are eternal, one would be hard pressed to provide a reason why this passage is literal over against all of the figurative language used in the book of Revelation. In my thinking, it is just another way in which the apostle John is revealing his vision received on the Isle of Patmos.

The Lake of Fire (Revelation 20:10)

It is into the Lake of Fire that the devil, along with the false prophet and the beast will be thrown (Rev. 20:10). It is to this text that many will turn to argue that they will be tormented day and night forever and ever.

This information is in contrast to the word given in Isaiah 14:12–15 and Ezekiel 28:19 which declares the total end and ruin of Satan. According to Ezekiel, he will be destroyed and be no more (Ezek. 28:19).

The use of figurative language is common to this text as seen in the description of Gog and Magog who are as numerous as the "*sand of the seashore*" (Rev. 20:8). The idea that this army will be equal to the number of the sands of the seashore is not expected. It is written this way for emphasis. In a similar way, the devil will be tortured forever and ever, suggesting a long time, but as Ezekiel has spoken concerning the devil, he will come to an end and be no more.

APPENDIX B

Chapter Study Questions

<u>STUDY QUESTIONS</u>

Chapter 1—Truth Handles

1. Identify questions that you have posed concerning the Bible, but have never followed your question through to the point of framing an answer from the Scriptures.

2. Make a list of biblical or life issues that sometimes cause controversy within the Christian community (i.e., inerrancy, nature of man, hell, heaven, homosexuality)

3. In your opinion, how important is it to "correctly handle" the word of God? If important, how does one go about doing this?

4. Discuss ways in which you have seen the misinterpretation or mishandling of God's word.

5. Name the top three guidelines that you think are important when it comes to interpreting the word of God (i.e., let Scripture interpret Scripture).

STUDY QUESTIONS

Chapter 2—The Beginning of the End

1. Review the creation narratives in Genesis and describe what you think regarding the phrase, *"It was good."*

2. In your opinion, why would God prohibit Adam and Eve from eating of the tree of the knowledge of good and evil (Gen. 2:17)?

3. Identify from the creation and fall of man texts found in Genesis those places where the subject of mortality or immortality are presented.

4. Describe what you believe to be the predominant characteristics of mortality and immortality.

5. Discuss Satan's behavior in the garden. What in your opinion was Satan's strategy in dealing with Adam and Eve?

STUDY QUESTIONS

Chapter 3—The Other Tree

1. Do you believe that God allowed Adam and Eve to eat of the tree of life prior to their sin? What biblical support do you have for or against your opinion?

2. Explain why God decided to ban Adam and Eve from the garden following their sin. What, if anything, does this text say about man's nature outside the garden?

3. If the tree of life provided the possibility of living forever in sin, what might it mean to die without having eaten of the tree of life?

4. Is there any significance to the passages telling of how God drove Adam and Eve from the garden? What does this word suggest in terms of man's reaction to God's decision to banish them?

5. How did Adam and Eve's lives change once they were outside of the garden?

STUDY QUESTIONS

Chapter 4—Good Dirt—Bad Dirt

1. What is the significance of Satan's statement, "*You will not surely die*," in relationship to God's pronouncement of death upon Adam and Eve as a result of their sin?

2. In your opinion, based on the text, what was man's nature like prior to God breathing into Adam the breath of life (Gen. 2:7)?

3. Respond to David's words in Psalm 146:3–4 as it pertains to the subject of death and the afterlife.

4. What do you think it means that Adam was described following his creation as "good?" What are the implications of this pronouncement?

5. What does it mean when Paul states in 1 Timothy 6:16 concerning God that he "alone is immortal?" If God alone has immortality, what about man? What are the implications of your conclusion?

STUDY QUESTIONS

Chapter 5—Truth and Consequences

1. Describe as much as you can about Adam and Eve's life experience outside of the garden.

2. Discuss the differences between the terms die and perish.

3. In light of your discussion above (question #2), discuss the implications of John 3:16 and its use of the word perish.

4. 2 Timothy 1:10 states that Jesus "*brought life and immortality to light through the gospel.*" What does this mean and how did Jesus do this through his life and the gospel.

5. Contrast man's creation as "*in the image*" with Christ being "*the image*" of God (1 Cor. 11:7; Col. 1:15).

STUDY QUESTIONS

Chapter 6—Dead Men Talking

1. List all of the words with which you are familiar that describe death (biblical and nonbiblical).

2. Explain how the Bible uses the term sleep to describe death (John 11).

3. According to John 11:39, what does Mary's statement, "*By this time there is a bad odor, for he has been there for four days*" suggest concerning her theology of death and the afterlife?

4. Do you think it is odd that Lazarus was silent about what he experienced in death? Why or why not?

5. If a person goes to heaven upon their death, what in your opinion is the reason for the resurrection?

STUDY QUESTIONS

Chapter 7—Friend or Foe

1. What comes to mind when you think of the word mystery (1 Cor. 15:51)?

2. Discuss the term "firstfruits" as it relates to Christ (1 Cor. 15:20). What does this mean in relationship to mankind?

3. Consider the significance of Paul's words in 1 Corinthians 15:22–24 concerning the sequence of events at the time of the resurrection.

4. Share with your group the experience and thoughts you have had while attending funerals. What theological views have you noticed?

5. Discuss the belief by some who think that man is naturally immortal in contrast with Paul's teaching that people will be changed from a mortal being into an immortal being at the time of the resurrection (1 Cor. 15:53).

STUDY QUESTIONS

Chapter 8—Dead Silence

1. What do you make of those who proclaim that they have had an out of the body experience? Find some material about this subject and compare it with the Scriptures.

2. Discuss the idea of paradise or heaven without Jesus being present.

3. Comment on Psalm 115:17 and Psalm 88:11–12 in light of the common belief that one immediately goes to heaven when they die. What do you think?

4. Share your thoughts after reading Hebrews 11:39–40 with your group. What does this text suggest concerning the destiny of people at the point of death?

5. What was the reason the chief priests wanted to kill Lazarus (John 12:9–10)? What is the evidence for your position?

STUDY QUESTIONS

Chapter 9—Join the Club

1. To be dead and alive at the same time sounds like a "spiritual oxymoron." What do you think?

2. If death is no longer an enemy for mankind, why is death the last great enemy destroyed at the time of the second coming (1 Cor. 15:26)?

3. Explain why Jesus has to return to get believers (John 14:1–4) if believers are already with him in paradise?

4. How important is it for a believer to have a "body" to enter the kingdom of God (1 Cor. 15:50ff)? Compare this in relationship to those who proclaim that the real man is spiritual.

5. Discuss the relationship between the biblical terms eternal life and immortality.

STUDY QUESTIONS

Chapter 10—Perish the Thought!

1. If God sent Jesus into the world so people would not perish, does this mean that people will perish if they do not believe? If so, what happens when something perishes?

2. Discuss the similarities and differences between the words dying and perishing.

3. Discuss the biblical differences between hell (*Hades*) and hell (*Gehenna*).

4. Share with your group your thoughts concerning Jesus's use of the word *Gehenna* as he describes hell as a place of judgment.

5. Talk openly about Jude 7 and its use of the words "eternal fire," that no longer burns. In your opinion, what does this mean? Discuss with your group your thoughts on the author's comments on how eternal is used in the Bible.

STUDY QUESTIONS

Chapter 11—Hell, What Do I Know?

1. What have you heard about Luke 16 pertaining to the nature of hell?

2. Discuss the nature of a parable. Does Luke 16, in your opinion, fit within the parameters of a parable? Why or why not?

3. Jesus always uses the word *Gehenna* when talking about hell and judgment. How do you explain that in this story the word *Hades* is used, which means grave, instead of *Gehenna*?

4. Read Luke 17:1–3 and discuss the warning Jesus gives to his listeners. How does this meaning relate to the story in Luke 16?

5. What is the significance of the statement found in Luke 16:31?

STUDY QUESTIONS

Chapter 12—A Grave Situation

1. Read Luke 23:43 and John 20:10–17 and compare your findings and discuss any theological implications.

2. Consider with your group the various options for interpreting Jesus's statement to the thief on the cross ("*I tell you truth, today you will be with me in paradise*")?

3. Jesus says in John 17:13 that he was going to return to the Father. When, exactly did he do this?

4. Comment on Jesus's statement in John 20:17, which says that he had not yet returned to his Father (only three days after the Crucifixion)?

5. Talk about the significance that David's body decayed, yet Jesus's body did not (Acts 13:36–37).

STUDY QUESTIONS

Chapter 13—To Die or Not to Die?

1. Name some songs you sing that express theology you don't accept.

2. How does the *"god of this age"* (2 Cor. 4:4) seek to blind us from the truth? What, in your opinion, are some of Satan's best-used strategies for blinding us from the truth?

3. Paul describes the second coming of Christ as the believer's blessed hope (Titus 2:13). In what ways is this second coming the blessed hope?

4. The author speaks of "bad theology." Where, in you opinion, do we receive most of our bad theology from today? What can a believer do to protect himself/herself from bad theology?

5. Do you remember when you last faced a sense of your own mortality? If so, share this with your group.

STUDY QUESTIONS

Chapter 14—For Better or Worse

1. Discuss among your group some of the "ditties" that you have heard or used to express the depth of your love for your family or mate (go ahead, be silly).

2. Is John the apostle correct when he states that "*God has given us eternal life, and this life is in his Son? He who has the Son has life; he who does not have the Son does not have life*" (1 John 5:11–12)? Describe in detail the kind of life John is talking about in this passage.

3. In 1 Timothy 1:17 the apostle Paul uses a number of adjectives to describe the nature of God. Read this passage and discuss these adjectives. How in your opinion is God different than mankind? How are we like him?

4. The Bible presents salvation of man on the basis of one condition. In your opinion, what is this condition? How does this condition relate to man's eternal destiny?

5. Discuss the importance of the resurrection in regards to man receiving the gift of immortality.

STUDY QUESTIONS

Chapter 15—For Heaven's Sake!

1. Describe your concept of heaven and how you arrived at this view.

2. What role, if any, do you think culture and other nonbiblical sources have on influencing the modern day view of heaven?

3. Revelation 21:1–4 describes the New Jerusalem coming down to man. How does this fit with the common teaching that people go "up" to heaven? If it doesn't fit, what does it mean?

4. What, if any, are the implications of the Bible's teaching that the present heavens and earth will be destroyed by fire and replaced by new ones (2 Peter 3:10–13; Rev. 21:1–4)?

5. Paul says in 1 Corinthians 2:9 that God is preparing a place (John 14:1–4) that no one has seen. If this is true, how can people be in heaven now? What do you think?

STUDY QUESTIONS

Chapter 16—On One Condition

1. John writes in his first epistle that to not have the Son of God (believe by faith) is to not have life (1 John 5:11–12). What does John mean by these words, "Does not have life?"

2. Paul tells Timothy that God alone is immortal (1 Tim. 6:16). What does this statement imply regarding the nature of man?

3. According to Paul, God lives in unapproachable light. Explain how man can be in his presence immediately after death if he is still mortal, having not yet received the gift of immortality that will be given at the resurrection (1 Cor. 15)?

4. Consider the resurrection of Christ and discuss how important it is in terms of what happens to believers at the time of the second coming?

5. In your opinion, will man be re-embodied (physical body put back together) at the second coming, or changed into a new body fit for the kingdom of God? What is the justification for your answer? And, why is this important?

STUDY QUESTIONS

Chapter 17—Life Only in Christ

1. Discuss the saying, "You can learn a lot by thinking" in relationship to building a biblical theology?

2. The idea that many Christians today could hold a view of man's nature that fails to match the biblical evidence is a hard pill to swallow for most. What are some of your thoughts about this possibility?

3. The idea of "life only in Christ" is seen throughout the pages of the Bible. What are some of the implications of this belief for the eternal destiny of mankind?

4. Discuss the possibility of changing your view on a theological position which has been held all of your life. Would you be willing to make such a change? Has anything in this study made you think that you need to consider such a change?

5. Do you believe that man can be immortal apart from God imparting this gift at the time of the second coming of Christ? If so, how?

APPENDIX C

Scriptural Reference Index

15:47	28
15:49	74
15:50	28, 62, 67, 99
15:51	16, 67, 97
15:51–54	75
15:52	55
15:52–54	73
15:53	20, 67, 72, 79, 97
15:54	28, 45, 68
15:54–55	46, 54
15:54–57	20, 54–56

2 Corinthians

4:4	54, 103
4:4b	54
4:6	54
4:17	54
5:1	54
5:8–10	52
5:9	54

Ephesians

3:11	32

Philippians

1:18	51
1:18–25	51, 52
1:19	51
1:21	51, 52
1:21–23	48
1:23	50, 51

1:27	52
3:9	50
3:9–11	51
3:10	50
3:12	51
3:20	51, 64, 65, 75
3:21	51
3:25	53
3:27	53

Colossians

1:15	95
1:18	88
3:1–4	64
3:4	51, 65

1 Thessalonians

1:10	65
4:13	17, 54
4:13–18	16, 17, 24, 27
4:13–17	38, 75
4:14	54
4:16	17
4:17	17, 28
4:17–18	55

2 Thessalonians

1:7	65
1:9	58
2:13	33
2:16	32

Selected Bibliography

Barton, Freeman. *Heaven, Hell, and Hades*. Charlotte, NC: Advent Christian General Conference, 1981.

Burch, Helaine. *Asleep in Christ*. New Berlin, WI: Bible Search Publications, 1999.

Chandler, C. E. *Immortalizing Evil*. Blue Point, NY: privately printed, 1997.

Crockett, William V. ed. *Four Views on Hell*. Grand Rapids, MI: Zondervan Publishing, 1992.

Dean, David A. *The Gift from Above*. Charlotte, NC: Advent Christian General Conference, 1989.

Dean, David A. *Resurrection, His and Ours*. Charlotte, NC: Advent Christian General Conference, 1977.

Fudge, Edward William. *The Fire That Consumes*. Houston, TX: Providential Press, 1982.

Fudge, Edward William, and Robert A. Peterson. *Two Views on Hell*. Downers Grove, IL: IVP, 2000.

Hewitt, Clarence H., and Herbert H. Holland. *Questions and Answers*. 2 vols. Concord, NH: Advent Christian Publications, 1964.

Lewis, Eric. *Life and Immortality*. Boston, MA: Warren Press, 1949.

Nichols, James A. *Christian Doctrine: A Presentation of Biblical Theology*. Nutley, NJ: Craig Press, 1970.

Wisebrock, George. *Mortal by Design*. Chicago Ridge, IL: privately printed, 2003.

Endnotes

CHAPTER 6—DEAD MEN TALKING

1. A contemporary song has been written by Carmen depicting in music the dramatic episode of Lazarus being "yanked" from the streets of paradise.

2. Luke 10:17

CHAPTER 10—PERISH THE THOUGHT!

1. The word *Tartaroo* is used only once in the New Testament (2 Peter 2:4)

2. Leland Ryken, James C. Wilhoit, Tremper Longman III [Eds.]. *Dictionary of Biblical Imagery: An Encyclopedic Exploration of the Images, Symbols, Motif Metaphors, Figures of Speech and Literary Patterns of the Bible*. IVP: Downers Grove, IL, 1998, page 240. Molech was the Canaanite deity to whom Israel, in times of apostasy, sacrificed children. Molech was the god of the underworld who had origins in Punic religion. In the times of Josiah's reforms of Jerusalem, the places in the Valley of Ben Hinnom where Israel had sacrificed their sons and daughters to Molech are desecrated (2 Kings 23:10; Jer. 32:35).

3. Please reference these passages for insight into the words "Eternal Life" (John 3:16, 5:24, 6:40, 54, 10:28; Rom. 2:7; and 1 John 5:11).

CHAPTER 11—HELL, WHAT DO I KNOW?

1. The word *Hades* is used ten times in the New Testament.

2. The word *Gehenna* is used twelve times in the New Testament.

3. The word *Sheol* is used thirty-one times in the Old Testament.

4. *Ibid*, page 5. This place is often called "Abraham's bosom." It appears twice in the Bible, both in Jesus's parable about the rich man and Lazarus (Luke 16:19–31). It is considered by some to be a synonym for heaven or paradise.

CHAPTER 13—TO DIE OR NOT TO DIE?

1. Found in the *Advent Christian Hymnal*, (Hymn #63).

2. Found in the *Celebration Hymnal*, Word Music/Integrity, 1997, page 111.

CHAPTER 15—FOR HEAVEN'S SAKE!

1. This information is taken from a 1999 doctoral thesis written by Dr. John Roller entitled, *The Doctrine of Immortality in the Early Church*.

2. This research was conducted by the Barna Research Group. These findings were revealed in a January 12, 2004, article entitled "Only Half of Protestant Pastors have a Biblical Worldview."

EPILOGUE

1. James S. Hewett, Editor. *Illustrations Unlimited*. Wheaton, IL: Tyndale House Publishers, Inc., 1998, page 482.

APPENDIX 1—PROBLEMATIC PASSAGES

1. *Tartarosas* is a *hapaxlegomenon* (appears only once) for the entire Bible.

0-595-33627-2